JINNAH HELPED HINDUS

JINNAH HELPED HINDUS AND OTHER REFLECTIONS

PRAFULL GORADIA

Vitasta

Published by
Vitasta Publishing Pvt Ltd
2/15, Ansari Road, Daryaganj
New Delhi-110 002
info@vitastapublishing.com

ISBN 978-93-86473-80-6

First Edition 2020
MRP ₹450

Editor by Veena Batra
Cover and layout by Somesh Kumar Mishra
Printed by Vikas Computer and Printers, New Delhi

CONTENTS

Why This Book?

The wide range of subjects touched upon in this volume may surprise some readers by their diversity. The one unity they represent is that of time. They reflect comments on happenings that took place during a period of 21 months (Gandhi was arrested by the British government in August 1942 and released in May 1944).

From cricket and parathas to education, events in Europe, Pakistan and, of course, India, have been discussed and analysed. I hope that most readers would find several topics of interest. I am not ambitious enough to expect all the chapters to engage all the readers, but I do feel confident that at least some chapters could interest many readers.

That Mohammed Ali Jinnah helped Hindus may well shock readers in India as well as Pakistan. Nevertheless, the book has been named after this chapter because in historical and civilizational terms, the finding is of enormous importance. It also delivers a message that there is still time if India wishes to correct its course beyond Jinnah's legacy.

JINNAH AND MINORITIES IN PAKISTAN

Jinnah Helped Hindus

THE VERY SUGGESTION that Mohammad Ali Jinnah, the chief protagonist of Pakistan as a separate country for the Muslims of the Indian subcontinent, who was successful in his quest of partitioning the homeland of Hindus actually helped them, would sound preposterous to most. It would, therefore, stretch credulence to suggest so. Yet, the fact is—even if it came about as a fallout of the march of history—Qaid-e-Azam Jinnah, the founder of Pakistan, did end up helping the Hindus.

Jinnah and the issue of religious minorities on both sides of the subcontinental divide reentered the political debate a few months ago when Pakistan's Prime Minister Imran Khan offered unsolicited advice to India on how to treat its minorities. Khan, a Sunni Muslim, perhaps must be aware that his country's founder Jinnah was a Shia, a sect now being treated as a minority. Some in Pakistan want Shias to be expelled from Islam.

That brings us to the Qaid. Jinnah was not exposed to religiosity. His father was a second generation convert; his grandfather Jeenabhai, a Halai Lohana from Dhoraji, near Rajkot, was converted to the Ismaili Khoja sect, led by Aga Khan. The Bombay High Court in its judgment of 1866, declared the Ismaili Khojas to be half-Muslim and half-Hindu (some Khoja womenfolk do the Swaminarayan *puja).* The writer has seen a signboard on a shop in Goa that reads Akbar Ali, Ram Ali & Sons.

The surname Jinnah began with Jeenabhai; Jeena in Gujarati means tiny. Mohammad Ali's first passport stated his surname as Jinnahbhai. Leaving for England at the age of sixteen, he had little exposure to Islam, except for a short stint at a Karachi *madrasah.* Once in London, he soon became a brown Englishman. After a four-year stint in England, Jinnah returned to Bombay in 1896. His child wife whom he had married in Karachi and his father had passed away. Family contact became limited; his three older sisters had been married. Jinnah took charge of the youngest, Fatima, and admitted her to a Christian school in Bandra. He began building his legal career as a magistrate at the handsome salary of Rs 1500. His heart being in advocacy, he soon took to pleading at the Bombay High Court. Most fellow advocates as well as clients were Gujarati Hindus, with very few Muslims.

One of his juniors, MC Chagla, was liberal enough not to mind Jinnah consuming pork sandwiches at the Ritz opposite the Gateway of India. "As we were drinking our coffee and enjoying our sausages, in came an old, bearded Muslim with a young boy of about ten years of age, probably his grandson.

They came and sat down near Jinnah. I then saw the boy's hand reaching out slowly towards the plate of pork sausages. After some hesitation, he picked up one, put it in his mouth, munched it and seemed to enjoy it tremendously. I watched this uneasily. After some time they left and Jinnah turned to me, and said angrily: 'Chagla, you should be ashamed of yourself.' I said: 'What did I do?' Jinnah asked: 'How dare you allow the young boy to eat pork sausages?' I said: 'Look, Jinnah, I had to use all my mental faculties to come to a quick decision. The question was—should I let Jinnah lose his election or should I let the boy go to eternal damnation? I chose in your favour.' (MC Chagla, *Roses in December),* as quoted in *Jinnah of Pakistan* by Stanley Wolpert. Former (now deceased) Pakistan President General Zia tried to convince Wolpert to censor parts of his book that talked about Jinnah eating pork and drinking alcohol so it could be mandatory reading for all undergraduate students. Wolpert refused to have passages from his book censored, even after being given the promise of 'making millions' off the book.

Jinnah had a younger brother, Ahmed Ali, a friend of my maternal grandfather Dharamdas Vora. Ahmed admitted to Vora that he enjoyed his sundowner, a taste and habit picked up from his elder brother. Ahmed was clear that they were culturally Parsi; they did not perform the *namaz.* Until his brother became the League president, they had no *pyjamas*, so convenient for *namaz.* The elder Jinnah had married Ruttie Petit, the daughter of a Parsi bigwig. Religion occurred to Jinnah when he became Muslim League president; lest Sunni Muslims question him about his not being cent percent Muslim, he shifted to the Asna-Ashri sect, the dominant among Shias.

In 1928, at the Congress plenary session at Calcutta, he got a rude shock. Jinnah, far from being accorded the respect of a national leader, was hooted out as he insisted on addressing the Mahatma as "Mister Gandhi". Leaving Calcutta next morning, at the door of his compartment at Howrah, he told his friend Dewan Chaman Lal who had come to see him off, 'This is the parting of ways.'

Jinnah was indeed done with the Congress; he shifted to London, buying an impressive bungalow at Hampstead. He practised from the Empire's capital, becoming its highest paid barrister. His daughter Dina joined him and entered a classy school. All this indicated that Jinnah intended to live in London semi-permanently. The Englishman in him truly liked the English environment.

The newly married Liaqat Ali Khan—a prominent Muslim League politician and later the first Prime Minister of Pakistan—arrived in London with his young bride as a stopover on his honeymoon. He telephoned Jinnah, who invited the couple to Hampstead for dinner. Liaqat confided that Muslim Leaguers in India felt leaderless and wanted Jinnah to return and lead them. But Jinnah wanted Liaqat to first check whether he would really be their choice. Liaqat did a thorough survey, visiting every provincial capital. Most local League bigwigs displayed virtual unanimity on Jinnah as the supreme leader. They felt the Congress was comparatively active, while the League was not able to do much. No one knew what their qaumi aim should be. They had no objection to making Jinnah the president for life, if only he would return and lead them.

Liaqat's feedback made up Jinnah's mind to return and lead India's Muslims. According to Ahmed Ali, it was only on his return that his elder brother had *pyjamas* and *sherwanis* tailored. To crown his Muslim uniform, he acquired matching headgear, a black Karakul fur cap. His portrait in this get-up appears as the founder of Pakistan on television, every time the contemporary leader addresses the nation. There, however, remained gaps in his Islamisation. Whether he performed *namaz* remained a mystery; his fluency in Urdu was a non-starter. English was his real language; the next best was his mother tongue Gujarati.

Elections as required under the Government of India Act of 1935, were held in 1937 in every province. Despite a separate Muslim and non-Muslim electorate, the League fared poorly. Jinnah now had to find a way to galvanise the Muslims. With no mass contact, his feedback was probably his Khoja and Memon acquaintances in Bombay. The ulemas as well as orthodox elitists fell for Dar-ul-Islam. A greater ideal was a "new Medina", particularly because with the abolition of the Caliphate in 1924, and the last Caliph and Sultan of Turkey Mehmed VI being exiled, nostalgia was whipped up for pan-Islamism.

From the days of Sir Syed Ahmed Khan, a 19th century Islamic reformist and founder of the Aligarh Muslim University (AMU), there was talk of Hindus and Muslims as two separate *qaums* or nations. Sir Syed Ahmed Khan in his speeches at Lucknow in 1887 (*Sir Syed Ahmed on the Present State of Indian Politics),* Consisting of Speeches and Letters Reprinted from *The Pioneer* (Allahabad: The Pioneer Press, 1888, pp 1-24.) and Meerut in 1888 *Sir Syed Ahmed on the Present State of Indian Politics,* Consisting of Speeches and Letters Reprinted from *The Pioneer* (Allahabad: The Pioneer Press, 1888, pp 29-53), unequivocally spoke of Hindus and Muslims as distinct nations who could not co-exist with each other. Syed Ameer Ali, a judge of the Calcutta High Court too had written on Muslims' separateness. Poet Allama Iqbal, as president of the League's 1930 Allahabad session proposed separate political entities. In 1934, Chaudhry Rahmat Ali, a Cambridge scholar, coined the word 'Pakistan'. The idea of a separate Muslim nation initially failed to attract Muslim majority provinces, namely Punjab, NWFP, Sind and Bengal. Happy to rule their own provinces, they saw no need for any change.

It was UP's Muslims who were most enamoured of a separate state, especially those of Aligarh and its university. The only segment that had thought through the idea of separation and its consequences were Bombay's Muslim businessmen who wanted to be free of competition from Parsis, Marwaris and other baniyas like the Shettys and Chettiars. In the words of Mr Muhammad H Habib, later head of the prominent Habib Bank, 'I would rather compete in business with Punjabi farmers than you baniyas.' He mentioned this to his junior business partner Ratilal Gandhi, who for several years headed the Bombay Pradesh Congress Committee.

In the course of Ahmed Ali's chats with my grandfather, one point stood out. In whichever field Jinnah operated, he had to be the number one, not second or third. He became the highest paid barrister in the British Empire. He ensured that he was made the Muslim League's president for life. In the Congress, he could not reach the top and therefore quit not only the organisation but also the country until the Muslim League claimed him. Jinnah, an introvert, did not compromise with the environment. He knew his mind and did not care for public opinion. On the contrary, he moulded it. For example, Jinnah even convinced the Muslims of the minority provinces, especially UP, Bihar and even composite Bombay, areas which could not have been parts of Pakistan. Majority provinces—Punjab, NWFP, Sind and Bengal fell in line late, less than two years before Partition. This only illustrates how Jinnah moulded public opinion so that he could find his place in history. Many students of the Aligarh University went to Punjab to canvas for the League in the 1945-46 elections. They were asked by the potential voters what was there in Partition for them. Their answer was: 'To create a new Medina.'

Pakistan was created and many UPites migrated to Karachi, only to find themselves unwelcome and branded as *Mohajirs* (migrants). Their leader Altaf Husain later had to flee to London. Much later, he went on record to have said that 'Pakistan was a mistake.' To conjecture, how then could Jinnah have convinced himself of leading the Pakistan movement? Muslims in the subcontinent were approximately 25 percent of the total population, and distinctly less educated than Hindus, Christians and Parsis. They did not own many industries, nor did they control business to any significant extent, except in Bombay. Whatever there was of Muslim wealth was in land, which the Congress party and its socialists were threatening to take over for the tillers of the soil. Thus, the community, in the foreseeable future, was disadvantaged compared to others.

It was easy to convince the gullible that for the Muslims the choice was "separate or perish". The clarion call "Islam is in danger" was convincing. Without being able to address crowds in Urdu, Punjabi or Bengali, languages most Muslims understood, Jinnah could sell this dream. A report by a young Pran Chopra, who later became editor of *The Statesman* is telling. At Jalandhar, Chopra was present at an election rally in which Jinnah, who was campaigning for the 1945-46 elections, spoke in English. When the *muezzin* called for prayers, Jinnah stopped and sat down on a chair while the crowd dispersed for *namaz.* He lit a cigar and relaxed until the crowd returned, and then resumed his address. Jinnah had no inhibitions and the public did not mind. The cause of Islam was greater than everything; the rest were details.

This is the height of delirium to which the Qaid-e-Azam had been able to rocket the Indian Muslim crowds. It is for history to judge whether his campaign was sincere or fraudulent. But one thing stands out—Jinnah's obstinancy in carving out a separate state for the Muslims of the subcontintnt did, albeit inadvertantly, save the Hindus from what could have been an Islamist catastrophe.

The argument merits scrutiny, no doubt. We, in India, celebrate anniversary after anniversary of India's independence every August 15th. A great many mourn it as also the anniversary of India's partition, which caused the holocaust of a million people and forcibly displaced an estimated 10 million across both the borders of Punjab and Bengal. There are those ultra-liberal Utopians who wish Partition had never happened, while the more ardent nationalists decry the sundering of *Akhand Bharat* (Undivided India). Then there are those who are realists; this group holds that Partition was inevitable. However, if one were to say that it was desirable, one would be hauled over the coals for political blasphemy.

Let us for a moment assume a hypothetical alternate scenario with no Jinnah or his campaign for a separate state. Had the British left without Partition, Hindu-Muslim antagonism would have inevitably escalated and finally erupted into civil war. The civil war would have converted India into a hotbed of unending sectarian strife. Assuming that the British had left India in 1947 without Partition, it would be naïve of us to believe that the Muslim League would have simply given up on its struggle for a separate state for the *qaum*. After all, what was Direct Action Day in 1946—upon Jinnah's clarion call—about?

Had Partition not happened, an undivided India would today comprise over 40 percent Muslims. Any honest observer of India's political scene would know how the community uses tactical voting to safeguard and advance its political interests. Such voting would have consistently produced a Muslim prime minister. Before long, the sovereignty of the people of India would have shifted to the lap of Allah the merciful, the foremost precondition of an Islamic state. This is not mere conjecture; doubting Thomases must read Pakistan's Constitution, including the first one of 1953, when the shadow of Jinnah still hovered. It clearly states in its Preamble that sovereignty belongs to Allah alone.

Without the handiwork of Jinnah in the late 1930s and 1940s, India would today be a democracy only in name—if at all. Not a prospect Indians would have looked forward to. On a grimmer note, India may easily have been identified by the global community as the world's largest terrorist country—and targeted as such. The energies of Hindus would have been consumed in keeping at bay a hostile population of some 50 crores. As a consequence, India, far from the incipient major power that it has become today, capable of reaching and exploring outer space and writing software code for the world's corporations, would have become the biggest battleground of medieval religious strife. Hindus who harbour any scepticism on this score need look no farther than the fate that befell Yugoslavia after the end of the Cold War.

Doing good to the Hindus was nowhere on Jinnah's mind when he embarked on his quest for a separate Pakistan. The Qaid-e-Azam's place has been reserved in history's hall of fame as the founder of one of the largest countries in the world. Nevertheless, in the pursuit of his space in history, he did end up helping Hindus escape what could have been a catastrophe.

Troika of Rights

AS THE REPUBLIC Day nears every year, one's mind goes to the Constitution and the wonderful promises it has made. The most poetic of them is Liberty, Equality and Fraternity, a vow taken from the central slogan of the French Revolution that began in 1789. The three words incidentally contain a contradiction between fraternity and the other two. Also, liberty and equality cannot go together. If a society wants to have equality, it has to willy nilly curb liberty. If say, the income of all citizens is desired to be equal or equable, inevitably the government must place a control on higher incomes—perhaps also add by subsidy to the lowest incomes. An extreme of this social desire was tried by the communist states led by the Soviet Union.

The contradiction between liberty and equality is best illustrated by the Hindu faith in *karma*. How can any society place control over good or better karma? And if a person's karma is excellent his *bhagya* or luck is also likely to be commensurate. How can the society or its government curb it in order to ensure equality among all citizens? If a person's poor karma results in the luck of his being poor, he could be subsidised or even fed and clothed free. But what about the other facets of good luck rewards? Then there is the risk of the government running out of money if too many of its citizens are unlucky, poor and need subsidies.

Article 15(1) of the Constitution states: The State shall not discriminate against any citizen on grounds of religion, race, caste, sex, place of birth or any of them.

This Article is commendable in insisting that there would be no discrimination on any ground—in other words, absolute equal treatment by the State. Yet Article 30(1): Right of minorities whether based on religion or language to establish and administer educational institutions of their choice contradicts Article 15(1). It gives this right and freedom to the minorities which are not allowed to members of the majority community, namely the Hindus. The minorities comprise mainly Muslims. Christian schools are in such demand that they normally face no problem nor do the linguistic minorities encounter any difficulties. Article 30 (1A) gives the minorities the privilege of being assured the allocation of land that is affordable by the proposed school or its society.

A more fundamental question arises out of this inequality. It was raised by Acharya Justice Dr Durga Das Basu (1910-1997), eminent Indian jurist and lawyer, who in his *Commentary on the Constitution of India and Casebook on the Indian Constitutional Law* rightly contended that a minority which deserves such special privilege or protection is one which became one (a minority) by circumstances beyond its influence or control. In the case of Muslims of the sub-continent, it is they who demanded a separate homeland, a Dar-ul-Islam or a New Medina called Pakistan. And it had to be granted by the departing British rulers and conceded to by the Congress Party because the Muslim electorate in the 1945-46 general elections overwhelmingly voted for Pakistan. To quote from Hamid Khan's authorative book *Constitutional and Political History of Pakistan*:

> The results showed a decisive victory for the idea of Pakistan. The League won all Muslim seats in the Central Assembly and 446 out of a total 495 Muslim seats in provincial assemblies. In Bengal, the Muslim League won 113 out of a total 119 Muslim seats, and was able to form a government with Huseyn Shaheed Suhrawardy as Chief Minister. In the Punjab, the Muslim League captured 79 out of 86 Muslim seats. In Sindh, a Muslim League ministry was formed. Only in the North-West Frontier Province did the League fall short of a majority by winning only 17 out of a total of 36 Muslim seats. These elections proved conclusively that the Muslim League alone represented the Muslims of India.

Partition was the single point manifesto of the Muslim League which obtained nearly unanimous support in the elections. The League's proposal, repeated by MA Jinnah and seven of his senior colleagues, was that there should be an exchange of population. Thereby, ideally, all Muslims should gather in Pakistan while all non-Muslims should emigrate to Hindustan. Justice Gopal Das Khosla ICS was commissioned to survey Punjab and report on the immediate post-Partition situation. The report was printed in a book entitled *Stern Reckoning*. The Justice wrote that an exchange of population was an integral part of Partition. After all, the vivisection of the country was necessary because Mr Jinnah said that Hindus and Muslims could not co-exist in the same country. If they were able to co-exist where would be the need for the division?

Article 27 of the Indian Constitution states that no person shall be compelled to pay any taxes, the proceeds of which are specifically appropriated in payment of expenses for the promotion or maintenance of any particular religion or religious denomination. The writer petitioned the Supreme Court in the year 2007 requesting that the Haj subsidy be withdrawn as the Constitution declares that India is a secular country. If, however, the government was not prepared to do so, he should be exempted from the payment of Income Tax. The subsidy was paid from the consolidated fund of India and the Income Tax was credited to the same fund. Four years later, Justice Markandey Katju delivered a long judgement. Its gist was that the Haj subsidy was like an expenditure made by the government comparable to maintaining law and order at the Kumbh Mela or on making arrangements for a visit to Mansarovar. To reduce or abolish the Haj subsidy would damage the edifice of secularism that Jawaharlal Nehru had so painstakingly built.

The following year, in 2008, Justice Aftab Alam decided in a petition filed by one Syed Intesar Mehdi that the Haj subsidy should be progressively reduced and discontinued in the course of ten years. The subsidy was not in conformity with the tenets of Islam, the judgement said. Incidentally, the late Syed Shahabuddin IFS and a former MP, had told the writer twice that this subsidy should be gradually withdrawn.

To conclude, I quote Acharya Basu from his book *Introduction to the Constitution of India*, (2002), where he makes a telling point:

> The leaders of the divided India incorporated in their Draft Constitution certain safeguards for minorities, notwithstanding the Partition, because they refused to concede on principle, that the Muslims in India constituted a separate nation. That India constituted one nation whose unity and integrity must be maintained was proclaimed in the very Preamble of the Draft Constitution of divided India. The Muslims who did not go to Pakistan did so with their eyes open to this Preamble and the safeguards for minorities included in the Constitution.

No Future for Minorities in Pakistan

THE PERSECUTION AND expulsion of Ahmadiyas in Pakistan began 66 years ago, with the first riots against them happening in 1953. Dr Atif Mian was an economic advisor who was sacked from PM Imran Khan's Economic Advisory Council on account of being an Ahmadiya.

Dr Imran Rasul and Dr Asim Ijaz Khwaja, both Sunni Economists, resigned in protest. Though a sect of Islam, the Pakistan orthodoxy expelled Ahmadiyas some 50 years ago. Pakistan was created as a Muslim land, a Dar-ul-Islam, a New Medina. Anyone who is not a Muslim is looked down upon as a non-believer or a *kafir* who can either be made to pay *jaziya* and have the inferior status of a *dhimmie* or a protected citizen. Or, he is offered conversion to Islam, or alternatively enslaved or exiled or killed. No minority, therefore, has a future in Pakistan.

If there was any doubt whatsoever on this score, it was removed by the cruel and expeditious manner in which Hindus and Sikhs were killed or chased out by early 1948. The recent killing of the Hindu girls can be added to this. In East Pakistan, the process was slower but equally callous. This religious cleansing was consistent with what Justice MC Chagla wrote in his autobiography entitled *Roses in December*:

> To Pakistan everything is communal. She cannot understand how Hindus and Muslims can live peacefully and have best of relations. Pakistan's philosophy is that in the very nature of things Muslims must hate the Hindus and the Hindus must hate the Muslims. If Hindus and Muslims constitute two separate nations, then the inevitable result must follow that the 50 million Muslims in India are aliens in their own homes.

Following the disposal of Hindus and Sikhs, the next round of minority purging was inaugurated against the Ahmadiyas or Qadianis. During the late 19th century, a devout Muslim called Mirza Ghulam Ahmad, of the Qadian township in Gurdaspur district of east Punjab, reportedly saw a divine vision. A significant number of people followed his leadership. The orthodox clergy, especially of the Barelvis and the Deobandis saw in this development a phenomenon of apostasy. How could anyone dare experience a divine vision after Prophet Muhammad had seen a series and based on them, delivered the final message of God? Thereafter, there could only be *Khalifas* or *imams*.

Nevertheless, the followers of Ghulam Ahmad continued to behave like other Muslims. For example, they pressed for the creation of the holy land as any other member of the League. Sir Mohammad Zafrullah Khan, an eminent lawyer, single-handedly drafted the League's Pakistan resolution of 23 March 1940. He had been President of the Muslim League from 1931-32, and from 1935 to 1941 he sat on the Viceroy's executive council. When Partition came, he was a judge of the Federal Court of India (the apex court in New Delhi). Sir Zafrullah was appointed the Foreign Minister of Pakistan. He also represented the country at the United Nations. This gentleman is only one example though many of his sect worked in the service of their new holy land. Yet, in 1952, virulent riots were ignited against the Ahmadiyas and Sir Zafrullah's house was set on fire at Lahore. He soon left and joined the International Court of Justice at The Hague, Netherlands.

In the wake of another agitation in 1977 when Zulfikar Ali Bhutto was Prime Minister, the Ahmadiyas were declared non-Muslim. Soon after President Zia-ul-Haq had the Constitution amended to formalise the Bhutto declaration. This particular amendment reads that Non-Muslim means a person who is not a Muslim and includes a person belonging to the Christian, Hindu, Sikh, Buddhist or Parsi community, a person of the Qadiani group or the Lahori sect, or a Bahai, or a person belonging to any of the scheduled castes. After the Ahmadiyas were officially declared non-Muslim in 1947, a new campaign began to subject the Shias to similar proscriptions.

On 11 August 1947, Qaid-e-Azam Jinnah gave his presidential address to the Constituent Assembly of Pakistan. He observed:

> You are free to go to your temples, you are free to go to your mosques or to any other places of worship in this state of Pakistan. You may belong to any religion or caste or creed, that has nothing to do with the business of the state. Now, I think we should keep that in front of us as

> our ideal and you will find that in course of time, Hindus would cease to be Hindus and Muslims would cease to be Muslims, not in the religious sense, because that is the personal faith of each individual, but in the political sense as citizens of the state.

The above statement was an affirmation of what Jinnah had told a Reuters correspondent in 1946 that the new state would be a modern democratic state with sovereignty resting in the people with the members of the new nation having equal right of citizenship regardless of their religion, caste or creed.

In this context, Farahnaz Ispahani in her book *Purifying the Land of the Pure* observes:

> This vision outlined by the founder remains unfulfilled. At the time of Partition in 1947, almost 23 percent of Pakistan's population, which then included Bangladesh, comprised non-Muslim citizens. The proportion of non-Muslims has since fallen to approximately 3 percent in the western wing. Furthermore, the distinctions among Muslim denominations have become far more accentuated over the years. Groups such as the Shias, who account for over 20 percent of the population, are often targeted by violent extremists. Ahmadis, barely one percent of the population, have been declared non-Muslims by a writ of the State. Minorities such as Christians, Hindus and Sikhs have been the victims of bomb attacks on their neighbourhoods, some of them have been converted to Islam against their will. Houses of worship have been attacked and bombed while filled with worshippers. Pakistan has descended to its current state of religious intolerance through a series of political decisions by Jinnah's successors.

The descent began in 1949 with the Constituent Assembly declaring the objective of Pakistan's Constitution as the creation of an Islamic state. It reached a nadir with the 'Islamisation' drive under General Zia-ul-Haq during the 1980s.

At the time of partition Christians thought that the division of India had taken place on the basis that Muslims could not co-exist with the Hindus. Moreover, Christians thought they were *ahle-kitab* (People of the Book), and therefore would not be harassed in Pakistan. Unfortunately, with the demise of Jinnah, the so called tolerance for Christians vanished. General Zia introduced Islamic laws which were openly against the minorities. The military rulers of Pakistan did nothing to control the violence of the fundamentalist outfits. Since then, Christians have been prosecuted and killed mainly on grounds of blasphemy. Salman Tasir, a minister in the Sharif government in Punjab was assassinated. His crime, according to fundamentalists, was that he asked for a fair trial of Christians charged with blasphemy.

Hindus and Sikhs were the first to be driven out of Pakistan during 1947-48. A very small proportion of them could manage to stay behind. Their population, according to estimates, is only about 14 lakhs. A majority of them are based in the Sind province. Many among them are agricultural labourers. In the last 20 years, their women and daughters have often been kidnapped, forced to embrace Islam and married off to Muslims. When their families have asked the kidnappers to return the women, the reply has been that they have embraced Islam voluntarily and married Muslims of their own volition.

The Shias were not to be spared. The number of times they have been bombed while praying in their mosques is legendary. The extremists like the Wahabis have expressed a desire to expel the Shias from Islam—what was earlier done with the Ahmadiyas. The next serious intra-Islamic cleansing began in the time of President Zia-ul-Haq. The obvious target of brutalisation were the Shias. Sunnis were provoked to look upon the Shia community as a worm in the Muslim apple of Pakistan. The required poison was manufactured in *madrasahs* associated with the Deobandi and Ahl-i-Hadith traditions. As written by the distinguished Shia scholar Vali Nasr in his book *The Shia Revival,* "The Pakistan *ulema* began to share Saudi Arabia's perception of the Iranian and Shia threat". The extent of the establishmental hatred is such as that a Sunni Muslim terrorist group called Sipah-e-Sahiba targets and kills only Shias, and is alleged to enjoy the covert patronage of the state.

Imran on Indian Minorities

PRIME MINISTER IMRAN Khan of Pakistan has offered to teach India how to treat its minorities. Is it not likely that when he said this, he was experiencing a flashback to his cricketing days, when our fast bowlers were not comparable to his country's pace attack? Traditionally, in the undivided India, it was Punjab that produced pacemen. The one outstanding name that comes to the writer's mind is Mohammad Nissar, the fastest opening bowler that the subcontinent has produced. Certainly, even now, their pack of speed merchants may have something to teach our players.

An Oxonian had once said: Imran is cricket and cricket is Imran. Similarly, Zubin Mehta is music and cannot be imagined in terms of cricket. So too, it is difficult to reconcile Imran's image with prime ministership. It is not impossible that while Imran was talking of minorities in India, his mind was on how to teach India to play cricket. Perhaps he needs to focus on the fate of minorities in Pakisthan instead. It goes without saying that he has not seen the holocaust of Hindus and Sikhs starting with Rawalpindi in 1947, nor does he know how his Christian compatriots had rejoiced at the birth of Pakistan only to subsequently regret it. The Communist Party had wholeheartedly sponsored Partition, later to beat its breast; it was simply eliminated by the torrent of Islam. As late as 2012-13, thirty-seven murderous attacks against Christions were reportedly perpetrated. The same year saw sixteen Hindus and three Sikhs bear the brunt of attacks by the zealots of the 'peaceful' religion who, of course, are committed to cleaning their land of all impurities.

The Ahmadiyas, whose hero Sir Mohammad Zafarullah Khan had drafted the Pakistan Resolution of March 1940, also had a taste of the glory of Pakistan. Imran Khan was not born then to witness the magnificent work done by Sir Zafarullah. Nor when in 1953, the latter's house in Lahore was set on fire, which induced him to flee Pakistan and not return until his dying days. The rest of the years he spent at The Hague in the Netherlands to bring majesty to the glittering benches of the International Court of Justice. In the meantime, the charismatic Prime Minister Zulfikar Ali Bhutto expelled the Ahmadiyas from the sanctified garden of Islam.

Another Ahmadiya who brought glory to Imran's country was Dr Abdul Qadeer Khan, whose thuggish doings in the Netherlands enabled him to obtain the secrets of the atomic bomb, all of course in the cause of *Khidmat-e-Allah*—the first Islamic nuclear bomb. He, too, was rewarded by being expelled. Well known scholar Farahnaz Ispahani in her book *Purifying the Land of the Pure* states the reality of Ahmadiyas being the target of Pak rulers. As late as 2012-13, according to her book, 54 lethal attacks against Ahmadiyas were carried out.

The writer was educated by two men. The first was his grandfather, one of whose friends was Ahmed Ali Jinnah, the younger brother of MA Jinnah. He relished Parsi humour and claimed to be culturally a Parsi. Although he was not a practising Muslim, he acquainted my grandfather with his insights into Islam—that, when a Muslim wishes to convert someone, it is with the best intention of opening a possible chance of the convert entering *jannat*. Only Allah could enable a non-believer to cross the gateway of heaven.

The second gentleman who taught the writer was his Urdu teacher who did not overtly suggest a conversion but did say that the future lay with Islam. Just extrapolate the progress of a number of religions. The Yehudis (Jews) have reduced in number and shrunk to a fraction of what they were. The Christians have scattered into many denominations. Many a worshipper in Europe has given up going to church. Christianity's priests have come to Asia, where according to the late Pope John Paul-II, there are innumerable souls to harvest. Contrast these performances with the progress of Islam, whose tide is continually rising.

However, all is not that well in the new Medina. Once the Ahmadiyas were expelled from Islam in 1974, it was the turn of the Shias for similar persecution. While they have been the target of the regime's hostility for years, violence against them began rising after the 70s. During 2012-13 alone, they were subjected to 77 attacks, including suicide terrorist bombings during Shia religious observances.

What to talk of Shias, the Barelvi school considered the Deobandis and Wahhabis outside the pole of Islam. They were liable to the death penalty if they fell within the definition of *murtad* or apostate. On the other hand, the Justice Munir Equality Report of 1954 had revealed that a *fatwa* of the Deobandis had called all Asna-Ashari shias *kafirs* and *murtad* for believing in the *sahabiyyat* of Hazrat Siddiq-i-Akbar.

In its 2013 annual report, the United States Commission on International Religious Freedom (USCIRF) described Pakistan's failure in protecting its minorities as having reached "crisis proportions". According to the report, "The government of Pakistan continues to engage in and tolerate systematic, ongoing, and egregious violations of freedom of religion or belief. Violations reached unprecedented levels", it said, "because of growing incidents of sectarian violence against Shia Muslims". The government also failed to protect Christians, Ahmadis and Hindus, it said.

In the overall climate of antagonism, Pakistan's blasphemy laws have exacerbated attacks on minorities by fostering religious frenzy, violence and persecution. The police frequently fail to record and investigate complaints, and justice is impeded by the biased attitude of some judges against religious minorities. Pakistan's national discourse, aided by its school curriculum, generates religious prejudice against minorities.

In Pakistan, there are a number of Lashkars who are anti-Shia, but the single-minded enemy of the Shias is the Lashkar-e-Jhangvi (LeJ) whose avowed objective is to cleanse Pakistan of them. They incidentally comprise about 20 percent of the country's population. Balochistan, which has many Shias, is a popular theatre of genocide. The head of the LeJ has gone to the extent of issuing a public letter declaring the Shias to be *wajib-ul-qatl* (ideally suitable for elimination). Despite this large scale genocide, Pakistan's government has admitted only 2,000 Shias killed over a five-year period.

The Shia-Sunni conflict has a dimension much bigger and beyond the borders of Pakistan. Sunni Saudi Arabia and Shiite Iran are arraigned against each other. Iraq is two-thirds Shia, while the just ended civil war in Syria was fought between the Shia-sympathetic government and the Caliphate-aspiring ISIS. However, the concern for India are the 25 million Shias in our neighbouring country. If the terrorism becomes collectively unbearable, where do they seek refuge?

Threats to Islam

DESPITE BEING CLAIMED as a religion of peace, Islam is under threat from modernity. First came the cell phone, which has become progressively versatile. With its help, virtually anyone can communicate with anyone else in the world at an affordable cost. The size of the instrument is small enough to be movable without being obviously visible. It is as accessible to the old and young as to women and men. Until its arrival on the scene, the average lady in a modest home had very limited access to information. The only possible source was the Friday *khutbah* (speech by the imam), whose substance could be obtained via the lady's father, husband or brother.

Earlier, the television had become an effective news medium for those households which could afford a TV set. Some households that could afford it, did not purchase one in order to discourage the family members from receiving news as well as views freely. Moreover, some orthodox organisations in some areas were reported to be asking their representatives to keep watch during the afternoons to discourage family members from watching television serials in which women were seen enjoying all kinds of freedom. No doubt, the television is only a one way communication unlike the cell phone.

It is noteworthy of the Abrahamic religions that Judaism has shrunk to a comparatively small number of followers. They reside mainly in the USA and Israel. Christianity has scattered into scores of denominations. The first separation took place in the 4th century AD when Emperor Constantine moved out from Rome and helped the establishment of the Eastern Church on the sea coast of the Bosphorus. For a millennium thereafter, there were no formal changes. Let us recall that many subsequent changes and splits took place between then and the 20th century. Christian churches were liberal and allowed sections to become independent. No undue resistance was put in the path of separatism.

When it comes to Islam, the law is so strict that anyone leaving the religion is declared a *murtad* (apostate). It is a crime punishable even by death. In order to minimise theological differences of opinion, questioning is discouraged. Undue distribution of information is avoided. The policy is for womenfolk to be taught enough to be able to pray but education much beyond that is not to be encouraged. The belief may be that the less one knows the less one is likely to question. Moreover, an uneducated mother would not normally know the value of education. Hence, she was not likely to insist on her children studying.

Television, the cell phone and the internet are all inimical to this value system whereby the less one knows, the less one would question. To that extent, a global village is a threat to Islam. The thinkers of early Islam were evidently men of vision. They could foresee the effects of information leading to knowledge and then thinking. And thinking leads to questioning. While the theology was being moulded, they did allow *ijtehad* (reinterpretation), which did involve questioning and debate. Differences must have arisen but were resolved for all the believers in the world to think, pray and otherwise worship, as if in unison.

After the first four or five centuries, it must have been observed that Islam guided by the *Quran*, the *Hadith* (traditions) and *Sunnah* (the life of the Prophet) was a complete shelf of theology, if not also its library of reference. No further change or reform appeared to be needed. It was, therefore, resolved that the time for *ijtehad* was over. The era of *taqlid* (orthodoxy) had begun and has lasted to this day. Those whom we call liberals in the secular world may find Islam unchanging, but if the Muslims are self-sufficient and satisfied, who are they to question?

However, the people who question began elbowing forward when Muslim leaders, especially in India, began claiming that their community was backward and needed support with the help of reservations in the services and separation of electorates. Until 1858, India was considered a Dar-ul-Islam by the Islamic world and Emperor Bahadur Shah Zafar sat on the throne of Delhi. Had the Persian invader Nadir Shah not robbed the Red Fort of the Peacock throne, Bahadur Shah would have sat on it. The rule of the sultans and badshahs over the greater part of Hindustan commenced in 1206 AD. Since Qutbuddin Aibak became the sultan, no non-Muslim ruled from Delhi until the East India Company displaced Bahadur Shah. How can the favoured citizens of this Islamic empire be backward? Does the secret lie in *taqlid*?

For those who were perceptive, the first threat to Islam was evident when the Muslim orthodoxy in West Pakistan, during 1953, accused Mirza Ghulam Ahmad of being an apostate. The Mirza had claimed to be a *mahdi* or a messiah. This was seen as an impermissible deviation from Islam. On the other hand, his followers known as Ahmadiyas insisted that they were as good Muslims as any other. The orthodoxy, who called themselves the Lahore Group, resorted to rioting against the Ahmadiyas. Their houses were set on fire, other properties looted, their men were assassinated to the extent that their pre-eminence Sir Mohammad Zafarullah Khan had to flee Pakistan.

The gentleman had served the Muslim cause all his adult life, to the extent that he had drafted the Pakistan Resolution, which was passed by the Muslim League in 1940. Zafarullah Khan also represented Pakistan as its ambassador at the United Nations and was also the country's first foreign minister. Another Ahmadiya who took grave risks for the country was Dr AQ Khan, who stole nuclear secrets from the Netherlands for the benefit of making the Islamic bomb.

A faith whose orthodoxy hounded such eminences and, eventually in 1974, expelled the Ahmadiyas from the fold of Islam was certainly a religion heading for a split, perhaps for the first time. After dealing in this fashion with the Ahmadiyas, the orthodoxy had tasted blood. Their next target were the Shias. This sect has claimed to have seen no alternative vision and are, in fact, the followers of imams who were blood relations of the holy Prophet Mohammad. The Shia sect, as distinct from the Sunni, began with the betrayal and killing of Imam Hazrat Ali at Karbala near Baghdad. There is no canonical difference between the two.

However, one thing is certain—that the lid over *taqlid* is off. In India, women had begun revolting against instant triple talaq leading to a recent law declaring it illegal. Elsewhere, there are women imams who run mosques, be it in New York or Tamil Nadu. In Saudi Arabia, they have begun driving their own cars. All these centuries implicitly obedient women were one of the pillars of the Islamic social fabric. But for the leadership of Qaid-e-Azam Jinnah, a Shia, it might have been difficult to achieve Pakistan before the British left India in 1947. When the President addresses his people from Islamabad on television, he has the national flag and the portrait of Jinnah on either side. Yet, some Sunnis butcher Shias, from time to time, and there voices are raised to expel the latter sect from the family of Islam. In India, a Shia leader, Wasim Rizvi, the head of the Shia Personal Law Board, has conceded that a Ram Mandir be built at Ayodhya on the spot where Hindus believe he was born. Sunnis are opposing such a proposal. This Shia change is not confined to the Indian sub-continent. Iran and Saudi Arabia are at daggers drawn in West Asia. The Alawis, a Shia sub-sect, and the Sunnis, represented by the ISIS, have fought a civil war in Syria. Islam is in the grip of a crisis. It is clashing with other civilizations in five of the world's six continents. Paradoxically, the religion of peace is at war all over.

OF JOBS AND SELF EMPLOYMENT

Working Round the Clock

IN THE 1940s in Kolkata, many a Hindu shop, whether of textiles or other items, was seen closed for the whole of every Thursday and half of Friday until 3 pm. Most Muslim shops in the Dharmatala Street and elsewhere were closed on Friday afternoons while the European and Anglicised establishments used Sundays and often Saturday afternoons for weekends. On the writer enquiring from his father, he was told that it all began with the Jews choosing the Saturday as Sabbath, a day for only worship and rest. Christians much thereafter selected Sunday as such a day. When Islam spread, it chose Friday whether the second half or the whole day. Hindus of Kolkata, earlier the capital of India, took the cue and reacted by using the Thursday and half Friday. Shops much later reduced their closing to only one day. In the old Hindu tradition, there was no weekly holiday as there were many festivals plus occasions like weddings, thread ceremonies, *shraddhas* after death etc.

Nature has created a 24-hour day broadly divided into a sunny part and a dark portion. But the two segments are seldom equal, varying by a few minutes to virtually non-existence of one part at least twice a year as in Norway, the land of the midnight sun at the peak of summer and of the midday darkness at the height of winter. It is people who have arbitrarily cut the 24-hours into two exacts, one for working and the other essentially for resting. This is virtually an unaffordable luxury especially for a society which wants to progress from poverty to prosperity. A poor country is one which has less assets and more people, which means that all the adults should share the few assets to make a living, and certainly not waste any assets even by their non-use.

With the advent of Rajiv Gandhi as prime minister in 1985, soon the five-day week was introduced. As a result, offices began to be closed for up to 130 days a year, the two-day weekend plus all the other holidays, festivals, and both Independence and Republic days. This means 49 percent or nearly half of the year is a holiday for many of the shakers and movers of the Indian economy. At the manufacturing level, the official working days are many more, but actually how high or low the productivity is in comparison with the capacity is another matter. There is a great deal of variation in the output as well as the true understanding of what could and should be the productivity in a particular type of manufacture. Across the decades from 1950 to say 1980, the late GD Birla was a legend especially in this context.

In those days, many a machinery maker recommended 50 to 58 percent as satisfactory output if the rated capacity was advised as 100. But the legendary industrialist used to exhort his industries to aim for 120 percent which they often achieved.

Productivity was one of the secrets of the house's success in those days of shortages. India was short of foreign exchange as well as still young as an industrial powerhouse. What applies to an industry is a principle which can be stretched to a country, small or however large. One of the several secrets of the German and Japanese economic miracles was their productivity. Whether it was yield per acre or production value per machine or per person or per hour, everything mattered. Given a high rate, the cost almost automatically comes down. Saving pencils, nuts or bolts is like conserving pennies, not pounds. The American saying "time is money" is very true but more so is that "time is life". In the national context, holidays are one huge cost, but few Indians view them in that light.

There are crores of cases pending in the various law courts. Why not consider running the courts for twelve or fourteen hours in two sessions per day? That may not double employment but certainly would help towards engaging more advocates, judges and staff with no additional capital expenditure. And, hopefully, the pending cases would reduce significantly. Delhi is actually short of college seats because not only students from local schools wish to join but also large numbers from upcountry want to study here. All one needs to do is to start a second session in most colleges. There would be employment for many lecturers, staff and reduced disappointment for aspiring collegians. The same principle should apply to shops, restaurants, even petrol pumps as well as factories. In short, the authorities ought to throw open 24 hours as potential working time and not the conventional 12 hours.

On the part of the State, there would be several essential duties to fulfil—roads, transport, street lighting and police-cum-security—treating day and night as equal and similar as do the Scandinavian countries. During the winters, there is no differentiation between day and night and street and other lights are on practically all 24 hours. Imagine how those countries must have worked and survived in the pre-electricity centuries. How cold and dark must the winters have been! Yet the people did not go into hibernation. Why then should we Indians as a whole have the habit of hibernating for half of every day, plus the whole of holidays? Especially, when we have a long distance to cover for achieving universal prosperity with less capital and fewer assets?

There is yet another angle to treating the day for working and the night for resting. Most of the country is more or less warm through the year. A venerable trade union leader told this writer that although factory shifts are eight hours a day, in our warm climate, an average worker is unable to put in more than three to four hours of work. When asked as to whether the night is better for output the answer was that if the factory lights were bright and the night reasonably cool, one could add say two hours. This is a reminder of how we should keep the climate in mind for productivity. For work under ambient (non-air-conditioned) conditions, nights are clearly more congenial than daytime when the sun is blazing, especially during the summer.

In order to achieve changes for greater productivity, mere action by authorities, whether government or private employers, would not be sufficient. It would be necessary for a revolution in the national mindset, just as for achieving Swachh Bharat everyone has to participate. If every citizen stops throwing garbage everywhere, the need for cleaning would become minimal; there would only be dust and other gifts of nature to remove. The reason for emphasising this revolution in the mindset is that the writer has come across few persons, including politicians and bureaucrats, who suffer from any qualms about the number of holidays that are allowed in our country. If it had been otherwise, why should a Hindu be on leave on Christmas and Easter days, or on Eid festivals? Or, what do Muslims and Christians do on the days of Durga and other *pujas,* as well as the miscellany of Hindu festivals? Why should there not be sectional holidays? Perhaps a practical way out may be for every employee to be offered a total of thirty days for all kinds of holidays/leaves and let him/her declare to the employer his choice at the beginning of the year. If in the same office or factory, different persons take leave on different days, the institution would keep functioning on most days without a lock on the gate on all holidays.

New Worker Laws

MY RIGHT TO work is fundamental although the Constitution does not say so. But then should governments, whether the Centre or the State, put obstacles in the path of whatever employment I can get? A recent stipulation is that my potential employer must pay me a minimum of Rs 15,000 per month. Unfortunately, I lost my father early and did not get an opportunity to study beyond class V. My mother asked me to do some work and bring home at least Rs 50 every evening. I did succeed for a few days, until the police threatened my employer with punishment for employing child labour. I was therefore out and back home to the distress of my mother. Today I am an adult; I am eligible for a regular job but no one I approached was prepared to pay me more than Rs 8,000 with the promise that I take a cheque for Rs 15,000 and return to the company Rs 7,000 in cash. The question is: do I stoop to this corrupt practice or sit at home?

Come election time, and young people are promised jobs. When I was getting a job, I could not accept it, legally speaking. Why are our political rulers so unaware of the gulf between laws made by themselves and the economic realities prevailing in the territories they rule? My boss, for whom I was working as a domestic help in exchange of food, clothes and an allowance, had tried to explain to me. According to him, this contradiction, from which I was suffering and many others too was a Russian baggage brought to India by Jawaharlal Nehru. Communist Russia, then known as the Soviet Union, guaranteed employment to everyone. This was a wonderful measure, very humane; unfortunately, it was one of the causes that led to the Soviet Union's bankruptcy.

Nehru was a socialist, so he did not go the whole hog in communism. His Constitution does not guarantee any employment to anyone. On the other hand, nor did his government try to understand capitalism or how social democracy functioned in Europe. More unfortunately, Nehru's successors, no matter which party they belonged to, did not bother either—to understand the syndrome that young people like me are the casualties of our leaders' negligence. Capitalist USA continually carries a percentage of unemployment, as do the social democracies of Europe. These countries have a variety of unemployment doles, whereas America distributes food stamps. On the other hand, India has welfare promises and legislations galore, without any thought being given to their implementation.

Over the last several years, the people have become quite conscious of the need for development. There is also frequent talk in cities of India becoming a superpower. We have abandoned socialism but are yet to think through an alternative. In any case, because of the size of the country, and its many people, it is difficult to discover a viable alternative. A bigger complication is the variation in economic development from region to region; there are varying levels of poverty and prosperity. Why not then give all the people full freedom to choose a job, an employer and a level of pay and perks which he can afford and the employee can accept with no controls whatsoever? This absolute freedom would offer a fighting chance that we may, before too long, reach full or near full employment.

There was a time when an unemployed person could live off his family, which in turn, depended on farming its land. But now, with increased population and the reducing size of most farms, this alternative for a man without a job or income is no longer there so it would be difficult to survive. Therefore, some income is a must. A low wage is better than no wage. The flip side of this situation should be an encouragement to entrepreneurs. Demand for handmade goods, especially in the affluent world, is believed to be limitless, provided they are not too expensive.

A Morgan Stanley report of three years ago had stated that India's labour laws force firms either to remain small, employing fewer workers, or to use capital-intensive technology. No wonder the share of India's manufacturing sector in GDP terms is one of the lowest among emerging markets. India's track record in creating productive jobs has been poor. How can there be any productive job growth if the country's labour market is shackled with regulations made 60 or 70 years ago? Another factor so far overlooked is that work itself is a training as well as experience. Even if a youngster has missed sufficient schooling, his early start in a job can offset the disadvantage to a significant extent. On the other hand, if he/she has to be without work for several years he would lose self confidence, learn little and lack experience, which is a springboard for building a career, however humble. An idle mind is a devil's workshop is an old truism. The imposition of a minimum wage ignores this old wisdom. In assuring one person a comfortable wage, it ruins up to nine potential careers. These nine include those who remain jobless merely because the minimum wage stifles the growth of the economy.

Laws and regulations like the minimum wage, say Rs 15,000 per month, touch only the organised sector of the economy which in India covers only 16 percent of the worker population. The remaining 84 percent are in the unorganised sector and do not get the benefit of government stipulations. On this basis alone, there is a strong case for lifting all wage stipulations. They serve only the electoral blandishments of a political party. Few political leaders realise the deathly effects of the minimum wage policy on the employment prospects of their young constituents.

Labour law is a concurrent subject under the Indian Constitution. Thus both the central and state governments have the right to formulate laws on the subject, which means multiplicity of laws, at times with overlapping jurisdictions. For example, there are 44 central laws and about 160 state laws on the issue of labour (source: ILO, 2013). Most are archaic, dating to the pre-independence era. There is an urgent need to overhaul these laws to attune them to present realities. There are multiple laws governing a single area. For instance, there are 19 laws governing conditions of work and industrial relations, 14 laws on social security and labour welfare, etc.

All in all, the appeal of this submission is for looking at Indian conditions through Indian eyes and not through a socialist heart. Most worker rules have a Marxist flavour if not an origin, including the British practices until the years of Margaret Thatcher. Many of India's laws are borrowed from British traditions.

Of Jobs and Self-Employment

SOME YEARS AGO, the writer introduced a father to the son of an owner-auditor as a prospective groom for his daughter. But the father declined because auditing was after all a business and therefore risky. About a year later, the writer received an invitation for the same girl's wedding to a youngster who happened to be working for the same auditor. I was later explained that a job was secure while a business had its ups and downs!

During the years the writer frequented the districts in Gujarat, he was invariably asked what industry or *udyog* could he help to bring. It was clear that the impression was widespread that the key to fresh employment was setting up industries. The unpopular truth is that a modern manufacturing unit is more an employer of machines and less a giver of jobs to men and women. By allowing for depreciation every year, machinery gets cheaper whereas the employees need to get increments annually. With technology advancing continually, the need for workers per unit of machinery or rather per piece of the product gets less and less. These mindsets, whether with regard to security of a job or the potential of an industry, must be given a go-by.

This is not to say that industry is not necessary for the economy to grow—it is, after all, the foundation of a robust modern economy. But if anyone expects it to provide a great deal of direct employment, he would be disappointed. The indirect jobs in areas like supplies, sales, transport et al would certainly be helpful to the economy and employment. The other threat to jobs is automation that comes with electronics and computerisation. Although not in a big way, yet robots are replacing some workers in factories. Then again, very desirably, more and more women are joining the worker market which make jobs fewer for men. So much for the second and third or service sectors of the economy.

The government or bureaucratic sector has grown to be very big and is already beginning to reduce or actually shrink. For example, the Post and Telegraph department is nothing like the giant it was. And yet, there are millions of young men who may go through life waiting for government jobs. For one, such jobs are traditionally presumed to be secure until the retiring age. For another, private assignments demand qualifications which not every aspirant has. In many areas of the country, commerce and industry are yet to be set up. Then again there is the issue of reservations which excludes quite a few sections of the people—the Jats, the Patels or the Marathas.

Yet, most politicians again and again promise more and more jobs. Everyone is for economic growth but that does not equal up to the creation of employment as most of the common youth see jobs. What is therefore necessary to inculcate is the idea of an economic citizen with a self engineered way of earning a living—be it as a doctor, lawyer, para-medico, shopkeeper or even a *pheriwala* or a peddler, but not a dependent on anyone for survival. The government's responsibility is to create and sustain the economic environment for the willing self-reliant citizens to have ready opportunity. The government's function is to govern and not provide jobs. The size of the bureaucracy need not exceed the demands of administering the country. The price of a heavy or a top heavy government would be either high taxes or printing currency leading to inflation. For example, something like 40 percent of the jobs in France are given by its government directly or otherwise. How long will the country survive as a prosperous modern state?

A great constraint of the European Union is the Euro which does not allow any of its member countries to devalue its currency. If, therefore, any member cannot keep pace with German economic efficiency, it either has to rationalise or head for impoverishment. The Soviet Union guaranteed full employment and this noble commitment was one of the causes of its eventually going bankrupt in 1992. Moreover, in the course of the 25 years since then, Russia has not developed as an economy. God forbid, if the country was not gifted with petroleum, what would have happened? A full employment guarantee sterilised the people's aptitude or potential for entrepreneurship. The spirit of economic self-reliance would do the opposite.

To refer back to setting up industries, it should be remembered that this is a globalised world. Almost every manufacturer has to face competition on a potentially global scale. Why not, therefore, also consider promoting institutions that do not have to compete so much, yet at the same time serve the immediate needs of the country? Health and education, apart from employment, are urgent necessities. Hospitals are quite worker intensive and several thousand of them are needed immediately if the common people's health has to be cared for. The Rs 5 lakh per family insurance scheme inaugurated by the prime minister will also be readily available. Pricewaterhouse Cooper in a professional survey has recommended that by year 2034 India would require 36 lakh beds. Today not even a fraction of these would be anywhere in sight. Each hospital would need several hundred non-medical persons and all the hospitals, when ready, should absorb millions indirectly and help to generate many jobs. The medical and para-medical staff would be extra.

If the Right to Education Act 2009 is to be taken seriously, thousands of schools would need to be created. Many of the state schools that exist are more in name and less in effect. Some have only a few teachers while in those that have more most teachers do not attend regularly. The result is that the students that graduate from them are semi-literate. Vocational polytechnics are the demand of the day; not to speak of colleges and universities. If only these are developed, the demographic dividend we hear so much about would be paid to the country. And if the institutions were set-up, their capacity to provide employment would be enormous.

Tourism, whether domestic or for pilgrims, is another area of neglect, although it has the potential for enormous, visible employment. The variety of sites to see, monuments to visit and place of worship to pray at in India are numerous. The Himalayas in the north have a potential far greater than Switzerland. The only deficiency is the lack of development and infrastructure. Conquering Mount Everest continues be a craze but those who can climb can take a jeep to Sandakphu at 12,000 feet and watch the tallest peak as if it was across a very broad avenue. The Kanchenjunga twin peaks are 80 kilometres as the crow flies from Darjeeling at 6,000 feet. The architectural jewels in Odisha can attract tourists from around the world. The Puri beach can potentially match many in the world but where are the facilities to make an American or a European tourist feel comfortable? Keeping aside employment and economics, it is a pity these Indian gems go unvisited, unseen by so many on the globe. South India again is a paradise for tourists and pilgrims but not with the current infrastructure.

Finally, agriculture also offers a great deal of scope provided we teach the farmers not only how to increase productivity but also to upgrade the value of the crops they grow. The late Prime Minister Charan Singh had written in his book *India's Economic Policy,* based on his field experience, how almost infinite is the scope of farming to offer livelihood to people. Israel has demonstrated how to farm in a desert with minimum of water. Unilever Ltd have demonstrated in their large open air pavilion at Disneyworld near Florida how, for example, 20 brinjals or tomatoes can be grown vertically on four to five square feet of land space. With the many small farms we have, this may be the only way of saving those who are today marginal or even smaller farmers.

Sarkari Jobs vs Other Jobs

JOBS, JOBS AND more jobs is the topic of the talk circuit with hardly anyone passing up the opportunity, whether in television discussions or written articles. Missing in this cacophony of "jobs, jobs and more jobs..." is the issue of income generation and, therefore, occupations that can generate real incomes. This, the writer believes, is a likely hangover of the middle class image of a good job—a white collar job, going to office from 9 am to 5 pm with a salary and an annual increment and privilege leave, with one's place of work preferably located not too far from where one's family resides. Governments, municipalities and panchayats still offer such jobs when their appointment resister happens to be open. Even for these state bodies, this traditional conception of employment is outdated if not altogether on its way out.

An increasing portion of present business activity is intellect inspired as distinct from enterprise and finance based endeavours. The primary machine to aid the intellect in today's time is a computer. This is not to discount the role of the machines in the manufacturing sector. But the truth, unpopular though, is that modern manufacturing units are more employers of machines and less a provider of jobs to men and women. One also cannot ignore the factor of depreciation, by allowing for which every year, machinery becomes cheaper whereas employees need to be given increments year after year.

Further, with advances in technology, the worker requirement is reducing; there is also increasing apprehension of the robots and such alternatives eventually replacing the human worker. For male workers, there is another cause of job shrinkage with more and more middle class womenfolk joining the workforce. When politicians at election time promise jobs, it is doubtful whether they go into details of such factors. Their audiences, the job seekers especially, think of such electoral promises as accommodation in the premises of offices and factories. Obviously, disappointment awaits many of them from the day after the promises are made. Neither politicians nor the people think in terms of employment as a whole, whether as shopkeepers, taxi drivers, or even vendors who move from place to place to sell their wares. In the world context, 50 percent of work will soon be self employment.

Traditional agriculture, once the mainstay of our country's economy and the provider of employment to the largest portion of its population, is no longer able to satisfy an increasing number of people for a livelihood. Employment is, therefore, the gravest and the most urgent challenge for today's governments. The term 'demographic dividend' sounds like music to the ears but actually will be so only if economists are able to find new ways and means of absorbing the new entrants.

Thus, a great deal of discussion in the country is over growth and development but little attention is focused on the specifics of employment. One possible reason for this oversight is residual effects of the inspiration India's policymakers drew from the Soviet era Gosplan with its emphasis on building heavy industry in the former Soviet Union. Five-year plans of the Nehruvian era were direct lift-offs from their Soviet example. However, the Soviet Union was a country with vast land spaces, enormous untapped resources and limited population. Employment per se was not a Soviet problem. We, in India, overlooked this, although it should have been our greatest priority.

What the imitation of the Soviet model did bring about in India was the creation of a huge bureaucracy to administer the Plans and other *sarkari* programmes, ostensibly with noble intentions. It did provide jobs to a comparatively large number of people. But in today's times, the government or bureaucratic sector has grown to be too large for reduction. The private sector has grown remarkably after the 1991 economic reforms, but employment in this sector demands qualifications, which not every aspirant has. Moreover, in many areas of the country, commerce and industry are yet to become a habit with the indigenous people.

It is time India stops depending too much on Western economics. We must instead innovate Indonomics. Our aim should be development in order to provide fruitful employment to many people and not the other way round. It should be remembered that this is a globalised world. Almost every manufacturer has to face competition on a world scale. Why not, therefore, also consider promoting institutions that do not have to compete so much, yet at the same time serve the needs of the country?

Nobel Laureate Amartya Sen has placed health and education as one great key to development instead of the traditional approach of pursuing prosperity for the economy and resultant enhancement of its citizens' health and education. We should adopt employment as our first objective, which in turn would lead to development, even if slowly.

Take for instance, tourism. It engages large numbers without the constant tension of automation and job reduction. These numbers do not all require advanced education or high qualifications. Moreover, tourism does not require high investments. One can concentrate on the country's ready assets like the Ajanta and Ellora caves, magnificent forts like Chittorgarh, or the Himalayas etc. True, Prime Minister Deve Gowda had told a reporter that India is too large a country to worry about tourism. He must have been talking in some specific context.

The next area to tackle should be agriculture where many farms have turned marginal and even unviable. The one immediate answer is upgrading of the type of crop to one of a higher value from the current cereals and millets. Farming can potentially provide for unlimited number of cultivators, but it is not an agro-industry that can solve the problem of rural employment. Sadly, this remains a neglected area in India, one that has also been the cause of much socio-economic distress.

Health and education, which are urgent necessities for the people of the country, are also ready avenues of employment. An area of beneficial investment would be the building of new and expanding hospitals, which are in any case desperately needed in most towns and districts. The outlay is not great and the employment potential is considerable. Hospitals are quite worker-intensive and several thousand of them are needed immediately. At present, there are only 0.65 doctors, 1.3 nurses and 1.3 hospital beds per 1,000 people in the country. The desired requirement by 2034 for every 1,000 people is 2.5 doctors, five nurses and 3.5 beds. The initial investment in this sector, particularly in semi-rural areas, would be in the region of Rs 10 to 15 crore for one 100 bed hospital.

Education, the key to furthering India's rise as a knowledge economy superpower, offers vast possibilities for employment as well. Thousands of schools would have to be created; their capacity to provide employment should be enormous. India needs 2 lakh more schools and 1500 universities and colleges. A whopping 220 million children are enrolled in schools, but 140 million continue to be left out.

Pathway to Mega Industrialization

THERE ARE ANY number of citizens who feel 'just as well that Air India has not been sold. To put the corporation on sale, wait for several weeks and then fail to get even one offer, however low, was a lesson for the government to learn. In fact, for a perceiving observer, the Maharajah story is a compendium of what not to do with a national asset. In principle, the Modi government was right when it stated '*jis deshki sarkar vyapari, wo desh bhikari*' (that country whose government is a trader, that nation would be a beggar). But the conditions in India are such as to require a relook at its policy of privatisation as well as future industrialization. The following is a bad example but nevertheless it is not an uncommon one. Or else, the bank NPAs would not have been so enormous.

Quite some years ago, an acquaintance of the writer wanted a project manager who would later be suitable for taking over as chief executive. The gentleman asked the writer to look out for someone he knew who could fit the bill. He explained his plan. It was a mini steel plant; its project cost estimate was Rs 20 crore, if the writer remembers it right. The machinery with which he could take liberty was quoted at about 10 crore. He proposed to jack that figure up to 15 crore. The financial institution would lend at least two-thirds of 15 which meant 10 crore. The capital was to be a total of 10 crore to be divided into half by promoters and half by so called public subscription. The first half was to be shared between my acquaintance and the State government, two and a half crore each since the steel mill was a joint sector unit. If all went well, he would get 5 crore from the machinery supplier and invest only half of that in shares. In short, the project would make a profit of two and a half crore for him much before any steel was produced! This is only an illustration of how the worst entrepreneurs think. The writer's reaction to the acquaintance was: why start siphoning before the project starts? He laughed and replied, "You are too innocent."

There is a widespread impression that privatisation of industry will deliver the goods which the public sector has failed to do. A fresh look is needed at this impression. Has the community of entrepreneurs delivered the goods to the extent it has undertaken, setting up industrial units of its own choice? Yes and no—it is a mixed picture. There are a few outstanding performances, some successful enterprises but there are innumerable cases of failures and closures. There are quite a few industrial estates for small and medium units which look like their graveyards. The quality of managers is not vastly different although the opportunity to be a committed executive who can work with his heart in the job is greater in the private sector.

The prevalence of ill-conceived project choice has existed in both the sectors. For instance, the government has promoted some quite weird schemes like a fruit export corporation or a photo film company. At the same time, some private promoters who were essentially traders, did not graduate to an industrial culture and failed. Corruption was, and remains, a common factor; the odd entrepreneur drew out cash as some corporations were favourite cash cows of the government, like the State Trading Corporation in its heyday. In skill, ideas and integrity, overall there has been no significant difference. Kingfisher Airlines and Air India are useful illustrations of the failure of integrity in the two respective sectors; in the latter case by ministers and bureaucrats. To add to the public sector came the sick and closed units from the private failures. The Textile Corporation is one example.

Neither sector is likely to deliver India's national goods which are necessary to take its industrial economy into the super league. Until recently, there was an imaginary hope that private entrepreneurs would help to takeover some PSUs and then proceed to set up large units. No one had the time to stand and stare at the private industrialists. They are either fully invested with no financial surpluses large enough to takeover more industries or many of them are sick, others are NPAs and yet others are trapped in insolvency. Moreover, not many of even the viable houses have bothered to inspire the faith that can attract unlimited public investment. The people at large have plenty of spare money to invest; in fact, there is a shortage of investment opportunities. Foreign industrial giants may not be in a hurry to set up industrial units with only their money plus the expectation of public subscriptions. The central government has to step in and play a financial or investment role. If that were possible without scope of government interference, foreigners could be attracted.

The reason why many a PSU has failed and others did not succeed was that we did not distinguish between administration and management or between the importance of disciplined procedure and of generating profit. The IAS officer knew the former and generally enforced it effectively but profit making was not part of the ethos he grew up in. In fact, in Nehruvian India, profit was a dirty word. For many years Jawaharlal Nehru considered many a profiteer deserving to be hanged on a lamp post. Often the new IAS batch began its career with a speech by Prime Minister Nehru.

Moreover, the joint secretary seldom learnt the tricks of keeping out the fingers of his pesky minister. And yet, he acted the role of a member of the owner family and tried to drive fear in the heart of the PSU unit managing director. Adherence to procedure and accurate accounting, as well as discipline, are important for all enterprises, whether public or private. But the objective number one of any business has to be profit, no doubt keeping in mind fair and legal practices. When it comes to large scale finance, a resort to the government treasury is virtually indispensible. The question is how to reconcile depending on the State and, at the same time, ensuring its non-interference.

The answer would lie in a synthesis of management excellence supported by State finance while ensuring the protection of every stakeholder. This is possible and it is best illustrated by quoting a live example and then describing a proposed model. Larsen & Toubro was for many years well managed by its two founder gentlemen and later their successors. Few common observers realised that 54 percent of the company's shares were owned by government financial institutions. The company was not considered public sector because the President of India had shares in it.

The Reliance group later came into Larsen & Toubro and the shareholding profile changed. Then they sold out and the company was demerged to split it into two; the profile changed further. Now for a model for the future—the government should confine its industrial investment to lending money at a reasonable rate of interest to its financial institutions like LIC, GIC and its subsidiaries, as well as banks.

Suppose a European corporation of repute wants to come to India in order to manufacture its line of product. It needs the economy of scale in production; at the same time, it may be reluctant to invest large enough sums to be able to control a majority share holding. The European company should have only 26 percent holding with a guarantee by at least 25 percent of institutional holders to vote with the company for a certain number of years. The rest of the shares can be offered to the public. If individuals do not subscribe to the full balance 49 percent, the institutions should be willing to step in. The European firm would bring with it its style of management, its technology, its brand equity, all for 26 percent holding. It should, therefore, be entitled to a royalty on turnover of product sale. Such a scheme should be open to reputable Indian corporations too.

If this model were to succeed to attract industrial growth, the present PSU's could also be dealt with on similar lines. Incidentally, provided the management of greenfield companies prove to be efficient and cut down on their gestation time substantially, the State could be well placed to find funds on a large scale through deficit financing. Delays in the completion of projects are criminal; they cause inflation and perhaps render the product outdated. This could lead to the unit going sick before it takes off.

Outsourcing an Old Practice

FOR SOME YEARS, opinions have been expressed that as a part of India's modernisation, worker laws need to be reformed. The opinions however have remained as good intentions well preserved. Meanwhile, economic growth has been slower and the outcry for more jobs is getting louder. The problem with the current industrial laws is yet undiagnosed and, therefore, the question of a cure has not been found. The writer has, in his endeavour, gone back two centuries. What was it then and what it could now be?

Outsourcing of work by business, industry, et al was first witnessed two centuries ago. The need was then of British traders who knew their trade but were utterly alien to conditions in Bengal. S Das Gupta in his book *Echoes from old Calcutta* wrote:

> Banyan is a person who either acts for himself or as the substitute of some great black merchants with whom the English gentlemen are generally to transact all their business. He is the interpreter, head bookkeeper, head secretary, head broker, the supplier of cash, and cash-keeper, and in general also secret-keeper. He puts in the under-clerks, the porter or doorkeeper, stewards, bearers of the silver, slaves, running footmen, torch and french light-carriers, palanquin-bearers, and all the long tribe of under servants, for whose honesty he is deemed answerable, and he conducts all the trade of his master, to whom, unless pretty well acquainted with the country languages, it is difficult for any of the natives to obtain access. In short, he possesses singly many more powers over his master than can be assumed by any young spendthrifts, stewards, moneylenders, and mistresses all together.

The cause originated in the demands justified by the Industrial Disputes Act, 1946, which was incidentally like a parting gift to India before the British rulers departed for good. They meant well, especially when one thinks of the arbitrary, exploitative behaviour of the employers in the early decades of the twentieth century and before. No one, however, could have foreseen the effects of the legislation in the context of militant trade unions of the later decades. The militancy was not confined to Kerala and West Bengal but also prevailed in Maharashtra, as well as Haryana. The north was marked by muscle whereas the Mumbai region produced more interesting varieties including monetary militancy.

For example, a union was led by one RJ Mehta which lent money sufficient to keep the body and soul together of the worker members through the entire strike period. The workers, therefore, did not get impatient to settle with the employers.

The loans were recovered with reasonable interest from the hefty increments Mehta squeezed from the management. Plus he took from the workers a large share of the increments for the first one year of the agreement. In Mehta-led agitations and strikes, no violence took place! The tactics, including the ultimate personal violence adopted by Datta Samant, a medical doctor, were again unique. The managements had mostly no answer but to surrender to the demands. Some of the enterprises collapsed after a time, so vexations became the workers' pay and perks.

To amend substantially the ID Act at this stage would be difficult; the trade unions have by now too many vested interests in the legislation. Even the affected workers would not like any undue changes. It is, therefore, best to frame a new law as an alternative to the ID Act. New projects could easily opt for the new law under which the workers are employed. For the established industries, let them carry on under the ID Act. When their three, four or five contracts between the workers and employers expire, let the managements tempt or persuade the unions to sign the new contracts under the new Act. If not, carry on and renew their agreements under the old law.

From the workers' viewpoint, under the old or current law, the statutory or retiring dues are not adequately protected, especially if the employer company were to close down prematurely. They may or may not get their gratuity, leave encashment or even the full provident fund. Under the new bankruptcy laws that have been recently brought, there may be quite a few quick and urgent closures. The first step the alternative legislation should take is to plug this probable misfortune. The safest way to do so would be to give say a separate bank draft of 25 percent of the monthly salary or wages every month. This draft should not be cashable for five years so that the employee cannot spend it immediately but willy nilly has to preserve it as a genuine saving.

The second feature of the new law should be that the wage be gross or all-inclusive and therefore without odds and ends in perquisites. This would enhance the worker's savings paid as part of the 25 percent draft. Thirdly, the appointment would be terminable with a month's notice. This would encourage entrepreneurs to promote worker intensive projects, also seasonal businesses without fear of being burdened with employees without work to allot subsequently. This fear keeps many a medium or bigger size employment intensive project from seeing the light of day. This is sad especially for the lesser educated or trained men and women. These are just the young people who need a break, an opportunity to learn a vocation on the job and prove that they can also 'do it'.

This writer is an example; he had a total of only eight years formal education. Had he not got an early break, he might have had to live with being a clerk, or even a peon. There is today many a job being advertised, especially by public sector corporations, which however insist on the applicants being, say, graduates. Yet there could be a good number of classes X and XII pass boys and girls who may prove brighter than the graduates. We also need to remember that there are a large number of schools and colleges which need to come up in the standard of education that they need to impart. The candidates consequently also vary a great deal in the quality of what they know although they hold respectable degree cards. The new law we make should take into account all these sociological realities and not just confine itself to the terms of employment.

The old or the current law is not merely obsolete but also

indulgent. For example, it permitted trade unions to pressurise managements to employ more workers than necessary. One way was to assign designations to them. Say, a gum carrier in a cigarette factory. His department would require a refill every 45 minutes, a piece of work which would take him say ten minutes at a time, eleven times in the course of an eight hour shift. Thus the gum carrier had say two hours work. The other six hours, he sat around without work. Another example, to unload a wagon of tobacco, there were gangs of 14 workers. In case two or three of the particular gang members were absent, the manager could not borrow substitutes from the next gang. He had to take on temporary workers while the next six gangs merely twiddled their thumbs. Quite extraordinary as it may sound, most factory managers had to collect, by deducting from the wages, the trade union subscription of every worker. The intention was to bind every worker to the union which, in turn, often agitated against the company. This arrangement is called 'check off'. So incongruous can be the results of a law when it is cunningly twisted.

Failure of State Capitalism

IN HIS COLUMN, 'Withering Heights', Govind Bhattacharjee (*The Statesman*, 21 January 2019) has highlighted India's most gigantic scam. Privatisation is not its panacea. How many private industrial houses do we have who would be liquid enough to pay and acquire public sector units? And even the liquid ones might not all have the confidence to get involved in units which could be over staffed. Work culture cultivated in para-governmental organisations would also be difficult to change for many a private management. Whither lies the way out? The writer believes that a beginning would be best made by making all interested Indians aware of why the country embarked on this journey of public undertakings in the first place.

The root reason was twofold. One was the ideological inclination of the then Prime Minister Jawaharlal Nehru whose faith in socialism, whether Soviet or Fabian, made it easy to push state ownership of the means of production. Apart from him and many a leader of the time, the academic environment too was Left leaning. Capitalism was associated with the West as well as imperialism. Many were psychologically anti-West due to the British rule. Marxists, whether Soviet or others, churned out and distributed a great deal of eco-political literature. The capitalist leaning polities of the country took much less interest in propaganda. All in all, in India, it became fashionable to be a socialist. Even top industrialists in Kolkata in their social conversations would not hesitate to say that we all have to be socialist. How else would the better off people survive in such a poor country?

Such was the growing milieu in which the party in power introduced a socialistic pattern of society at its Avadi session in 1955 as the national policy. There was no significant opposition either by the industrialist classes or chambers of commerce. No political party, except the Bharatiya Jana Sangh, had a contrarian view. Jawaharlal Nehru was thus able to unfurl the banner of socialism without any hindrance. From the viewpoint of industrialisation, there were a few resourceful entrepreneurs who in due course did establish large factories but these were for products of their commercial choice. There was hardly anyone with funds, inclination or the know-how to build infrastructural plants, like steel plants. Such contributions had to be made by the public sector funded entirely by the government.

At this point in time, awareness of one particular aspect could have saved the country and its economy; that is that investment and management are two different ball games. In India, to this day, this big difference is not recognised. Almost every entrepreneur believes that his offspring, preferably son, is best suited to succeed him. In most cases, he genuinely does not see the difference. His idea of professional management is to employ managers and give them powers but subject to the authority of the family member, who is the chairman-cum-managing director. It is true that over the last two decades there is realisation that non-investment management skills are necessary. But this awareness is still limited in the private sector and even less in the government, where possibly every officer might presume that he is as suitable a manager as he is a bureaucrat.

An officer knows his rules and meticulously follows the procedures; he has no yardstick of performance and can afford not to think about it. His preoccupation would be with how many steps in the ladder of promotion he has climbed and in how many years of service. There are no doubt exceptions, but those are by chance and not by choice of career or training. On the other hand, the average ministry would have no hesitation in placing an IAS officer as chief executive if one was needed as well as willing. It does not matter if procedure overbears profit so long as the rules are obeyed meticulously.

If this could be the flaw at the level of management, lack of accountability is likely to have been the bane at the top. Ministers are liable to change and the secretaries are prone to transfer or eventually retire. In the ultimate analysis, there is no constant factor to ask for answers; unlike the nag of dividend or the return on investment (ROI) beyond the dividend. So long as the auditor passes the annual accounts, he is happy. His is not to question ROI but only to clarify that the procedure has been adhered to. For him, profit or loss is a matter for the management to worry about. And a PSU has no ultimate, permanent management whose shoe pinches, if not bites, in the event of a loss.

What is the way out of this paradox of the need for results and the paucity of many giant and liquid entrepreneurs? The answer should lie in the President of India not owning the PSUs except financial institutions like the LIC, GIC or public sector banks. Ideally, however, even these should be inter-held amongst themselves rather than the President of India. Let the government appropriately fund these institutions, and even more of them if required, and let them invest. Let them be among the shareholders with the public as well. And why not foreigners as well as Indians? Let today's PSUs be converted into such corporate entities with professional managers appointed by their shareholders. Then leave it to each shareholder to be responsible for checking how his corporation has done every three months or so. Let the stock exchanges reflect the performance; the prevailing price of the share would be an important measure of how things are ticking in each PSU, whether central or state patronised.

If the government chooses to give a subsidy or offer a concession for a public cause so be it. But that must be granted as a sum of money from the state or central budget as the case may be, so that PSUs do not run either as zamindaris or as orphans ending up "as everybody's business but no one's concern".

An example of governmental majority investment and yet the company being run as a commercial venture by professional managers was Larsen & Toubro, until say, three odd decades ago. For years, the public institution held some 54 percent of the shares but otherwise ran like a normally successful company and there was hardly any wide awareness of who exactly owned it.

There is no doubt that the country still needs substantial industrialisation, especially of an infrastructural nature. The Ministry of Industries can invite Indian managers of proven record or even successful industrial houses, as well as foreign and multinational corporations of renown, to propose industrial as well as infrastructural schemes. Individual managers, if acceptable, would be asked to invest or find investment of up to 5 percent, whereas corporations should be expected to find up to 26 percent investment. Thereafter, if any more investment is required, the institutions should be approached by the promoters.

This would be one way of achieving rapid development without the need of the traditional public sector. With schemes suggested by professional managers of corporations, whether Indian or foreign, and approved in principle by the financial institutions, there should be a safe enough check on the merit of the proposal. With the Indian public also joining in to invest, it would be further reasoning.

Coming to the state PSUs first of all—local governments should be persuaded not to involve corporate or commercial enterprises in welfare or charitable activities. State governments, too, should be discouraged from investing directly in their PSUs. They could develop their own financial institutions as well as be free to approach central institutions, including public sector banks. Meanwhile, all sick units should be sold and if not saleable, should be closed.

We more or less began this article with an exhortation that investment and management are different ball games. It should be made clear more emphatically that business and politics or ministries must remain separate. They should restrain themselves from interfering with the other. The total losses made by public sector units, state as well as central, as listed by Mr Bhattacharjee, would total up to enormous figures. Add the cost of carrying these losses, and that would be another colossal sum. If only most of these monies had been deployed more constructively, imagine how much more progress the Indian economy would have made!

Psycho-Economics of Two Cities

SCHOLARS HAVE PROBED not only the psychological influence on economic behaviour but also psychophysiological effects. There does not appear to have been any attempt to explain why a particular person or the overwhelming majority of his/her community chose to pursue a particular vocation. The Calcutta of yesteryears has offered identical economic opportunities to everyone who came to the three villages of Kalikata, Sutanati and Govindapur as they grew over three centuries into a metropolis.

It is incredible how most of the major professions were pursued by specific communities. To start with, in the recent decades soon after Independence, British owners began disinvesting in their companies—partly due to their apprehensions about Nehruvian socialism, partly due to some violent incidents perpetrated by trade unions in the urban areas. One gory example was when two British officers were thrown into the furnace at the Jessop & Co factory outside Calcutta. A possible third reason for disinvestment could have been feared obsolescence of technology after the innovations seen as a result of the World War.

Whatever be the British motives, most of the disinvestments were attractive commercial propositions for buyers. Nearly all of them were bought over by entrepreneurs who had migrated from Rajasthan and not a single son of Bengal. The zamindaris had just been abolished and many a wealthy young man should have been on the lookout for an alternative occupation. This was important not only for the young men but also for business and industry in West Bengal. Some local ownership would make the enterprises appear to be 'ours' and not 'yours'. The feeling of 'ours' makes the trade unions view the industry more sympathetically. Not to say that people of the state at large would welcome everyone's participation. Why such a cut and dried, black and white picture only the psychology of economics could explain.

The expert's snap answer may be that the indigenous people of Bengal had not been used to taking business risks. But risks the people have taken and do take. A father with a limited fund often did not hesitate to risk half of it on his son going to England to become a barrister or an FRCS or MRCP or chartered accountant. The boy could come back and his practice might not take off. Is that not risk taking? There had to be some other reason to avoid business. Like a landlord might consider business an inferior vocation?

An equally interesting phenomenon was that there were reputedly over a hundred thousand people originally from

Gujarat residing in Calcutta. Many of them were traders, others were colliery owners and the rest professionals or in private sector jobs. Some traders were wealthy as were many of the colliers. Yet not one of these wealthy entrepreneurs ventured to touch the British bargains. Why? Should not the economists explain? Incidentally, members of hardly any other community except the Rajasthanis came forward to take advantage of the opportunity.

Avoidance of business and industry could be attributed to the fertility of the Bengal soil superimposed by the Zamindari system which enabled some of the land owners to have leisure. The time and energy this spared helped to facilitate the Renaissance which in turn could justify the claim 'what Bengal thinks today, India thinks tomorrow'. It should not be overlooked that West Bengal was the leading industrial province on the morrow of Independence. The only snag was that most of the industrialists until then were British. As they began preparing for their departure, the industrial decline started. Unfortunately, the fall was more precipitate than for a state's industrial economy to take a breath and recover. All in all, West Bengal has had to pay a heavy price for many of its people avoiding business and industry.

Trade unions also played their role in bringing down the economy despite being almost invariably honest. Paradoxically, their honesty brought greater problems than they might have otherwise. The leaders knew their science, art and craft like the back of their hand. They argued rationally, if not always reasonably. Most of the industrialists could not cope with the unions and unfortunately did not study their side of the art and craft of industrial relations. They did not give the subject the importance it deserved. The result was quite often agitation, strikes, lockouts, unrealistic wages and eventual sickness of many an industrial unit. The biggest of companies seldom had a Director who was familiar with industrial relations and left the portfolio to be handled by their labour officers. Incidentally, Human Resources exports dealt with executives and not workers. It is for economists to borrow from the discipline of psychology to diagnose the causes of this multi-sided failure at the cost of nearly a hundred million people of the state.

The enigma does not cease at Kolkata. It extends to Mumbai which was also a city founded by the British. King Charles II of England received the group of islands on the Konkan coast as part of a dowry when he married Princess Catherine of Braganza, Portugal, in 1662. What grew into a town and then a city was called Bombay which, initially because of being a natural harbour, offered enormous opportunities to whoever wanted to do business and eventually also develop industries. The Parsis came from south Gujarat; the Tatas transferred their ship buildings skills and experience to Bombay. They flourished as did differently the Wadias, the Petits and the Jamsetji Jehangir family. Also several other Parsis made themselves into big business houses.

Gujarati banias also followed with their acumen in trading, moneylending, broking in commodities etc. rather than manufacture. They made good money, were successful in their respective spheres and gradually became the beams and pillars of Bombay city. The Parsi big houses were much larger than the bania firms but the latter were incomparably more numerous. They followed the Parsis into establishing textile mills as well as other manufacturing. Hoteliering was not a part of their aptitude mainly because of their vegetarian inhibitions. However, they were generous with charities, building hospitals and starting schools and colleges. Then there were the Memons, Khojas and the Bohras who displayed their talent in money and business. The Muslim contribution to the making of Bollywood was enormous.

Another community which was prominent in the making of Bombay was the Goan. Be it football or hockey, the migrants from Goa were stars. Cricket was not neglected and Anthony de Mello went on to head the Cricket Control Board for years. For long years, the Goans led the catering services of Bombay. Chira Bazar was the mini-Goa of Bombay. The number of Mumbaikars naturally belonged to the Marathi speaking people. The upper classes took to education, both school and college, as well as the government services. As industry and business grew, they also became business executives. The common folk played a sterling role in providing the services as workers, supervisors and officers. All the communities played an active role as creators of what some have called the New York of India.

It is uncanny that each community dominantly played its own different role and seldom competed with one another, not to speak of clashing. Why? To an identical opportunity, how is it that each group responded so differently. Something to do with their distinct psyche? Or some other factors? Can the economists please answer? Why have they kept silent so long on the psychology behind different responses to the challenge—whether in Kolkata or in Bombay?

Education is Wealth

THE PRESENT DELHI government is taking a great deal of interest in the schools owned and run by it. During the year 2017-18, it spent nearly Rs 62,000 per student. For the current year the budget is a little less than Rs 64,000 per student. The total budgeted expenditure on school education is just short of Rs 11,000 crore or nearly 24 percent of the total state government budget. These are all very generous figures. Yet it is widely believed that most parents would like their wards to go to private schools only if they could afford the fees. Why should there be such a preference when government schooling costs next to nothing to the parents?

True, since the Planning Commission was set up, governments have talked in terms of rupees to be spent. Seldom did we hear, for example, of how many square metres of roads did the state plan to lay and of what quality. Whether concrete or macadamized? Is the problem of Delhi schooling similar? It is easy to take a head count of staff and teachers but so difficult to audit the quality of their teaching or their ability to engage student attention. Although the ratio of students per teacher is declared as 30 which is prime facie satisfactory, the ratio of non-teaching staff to the teachers is also important. Even in some of the older private schools, this is a problem. In the distant past, outsourcing was not in vogue and every required person was given permanent employment. Since World War I there has been a military method of analysis called tooth to tail ratio--the number of fighting soldiers to those supplying to and supporting the combatants. In the First War, the German army had one fighting man to four behind lines. In the same war, the British had a 1:10 ratio which made the latter army nearly two and a half times more costly or less effective. Perhaps the Directorate of Education (DoE) could benefit from such an analysis.

The monitoring of private unaided schools is a big burden on the officials of DoE. Annual or bi-annual inspections, studying the annual accounts and commenting upon them, checking whether over-aged teachers and employees have been retired or not are laborious functions. Again, what consumes the time of the department and quite often the attention of the officers is the fee increases by unaided schools—whether a particular school needs to increase its fees or not. The verdict usually depends on whether the school has funds to pay for the increase in expenditure or whether the institution has invested its past savings in any development. But the department's priority is not the improvement or the future; it tends to place greater importance on the mood of the parents, even a few of them, because they are the voters. Checking, editing or keeping track of such details of a thousand private unaided schools is a humongous task. On top of that there are up to 2,000 government and its aided schools, plus their one lakh teachers. Other employees are extra. After all, the school education budget of the State is nearly 11,000 crore rupees or a little less than a quarter of the total. In short, the DoE's task is colossal and too unwieldy to cope with.

The department functions on the basis of an Act of Parliament passed in the year 1973. The population of Delhi was then about a quarter of what it is today. The schools were, therefore, fewer and the problems were less. Look at the many categories of schools. There are private unaided and aided Christian and Sikh minority schools that do not ask for aid, then those that are called *madarsahs* which are fully aided. Not to forget language minority ones, some aided and others unaided. Then there are Kendriya Vidyalayas, Army, Navy and Air Force schools. There are those that are run by the NDMC and all those primary schools that come under the Municipalities of which there are three now. Lastly, there are the DoE schools, of which some are special ones called Sarvodaya—open schools which teach on Saturdays and Sundays only. In the words of the Parliament Act passed in 1973, it "applies to each and every school situated at any place in the whole of the Union Territory of Delhi". The Act is now 46 years old in these fast moving times. Most of the rules under which the department operates were also made 46 years ago. Due to the enormity of the work, the Court judgments are ignored. A hundred or more court cases which are precedents before applying the rules under the ACT get overlooked. If, therefore, a school happens to be aggrieved, it can either lump it or else go to the High Court. The result is more work and expenditure for everyone concerned.

To quote from the Apex Court in the TMA Pai Foundation eleven bench judgment, 2004:

> The private unaided educational institutions impart education, and that cannot be the reason to take away their choice in matters, inter alia, of selection of students and fixation of fees. Private education is one of the most dynamic and fastest-growing segments of education at the turn of the twenty-first century. State aid is not to be confused with State control over academic policies and practices. The observations referred to hereinabove clearly contemplate educational institutions soaring to great heights in pursuit of intellectual excellence and being free from unnecessary governmental controls.

In the case of unaided private schools, maximum autonomy has to be with the management with regard to administration, including the right of appointment of teachers, disciplinary powers, admission of students and the fees to be charged. At the school level, it is not possible to grant admissions on the basis of merit. It is no secret that the examination results at all levels of unaided private schools, notwithstanding the stringent regulations of the governmental authorities, are far superior to the results of the governmental-maintained schools. There is no compulsion on students to attend private schools. The rush of admission is occasioned by the standards maintained in such schools and recognition of the fact that State-run schools do not provide the same standards of education.

Each and every school in the Union Territory of Delhi comes under the purview of the Department of Education. The supreme authority to which the department is responsible is the Administrator who is the Lt Governor of the Territory. That is stated on the first page of Delhi School Education Act 1973 passed by the Parliament. He can appoint an Advisory

Board of experienced experts. The department is managed by whoever is designated as Director. There is, however, no mention of any minister and an elected government in the Act of 1973. Whereas lately it appears that the department is run by the minister of the government of Delhi. This is a clear symptom of how outdated the Act of 1973 is and how much a new law to replace it is needed. We have already noted the enormity of the work handled by the single department.

The Act was enacted for the purpose not merely of administering but for "better organization and development of school education". The very object of this enactment was to improve the standard as well as management of school education. Where does the department have the time to attend to such creative work—it has too much to do otherwise. How specifically the Act is outdated can be seen from Rule 37 i.e. "disciplinary measures" which includes corporal punishment by the head of the school in the form of "strokes not exceeding ten on the palm of the hand". Today, a teacher dare not call a student stupid, leave alone deliver strokes, as directed by the Delhi High Court! Merely to illustrate the obsolescence of the law of 1973, there is a mention of teaching as well as the setting up of schools as an 'occupation'. Today, experts talk of the function as the provision of wealth to the student!

ISLAM AND INDIA

Allahabad to Prayagraj

DISCARDING PRAYAG AND renaming the city Allahbad was a calculated insult to the Hindu faith, and to the sacred *triveni-sangam*. That the insult was delivered by one who has been promoted by leftist historians as a super icon of secularism, makes it not only ironical but also implies that virtually whatever a badshah, sultan or a nawab did is secular unless proved otherwise. Using the name of the only God, the merciful and the beneficent, was Emperor Akbar's way of targeting the sacred place of Hindus with his Allah. What an extraordinary imagination by the founder of Din-e-Ilahi, the blend of all religions, the ultimate in Indian version of secularism.

As someone who believes in the European version of the separation of state and religion, the writer nevertheless feels that to involve Allah the merciful and the beneficent in such mundane matters as changing a city name is insulting God as he sees Him. Even the worst iconoclasts who invaded India do not appear to have committed such a heinous error. For example, Akbar's great grandson Aurangzeb did not go beyond ordering Islamabad for Mathura and Muhammadabad for Varanasi. How could Akbar, wise and intelligent as he was, have resorted to involving Allah the omnipresent, the invisible, apart from being beneficent and merciful, in the despicable deed of insulting Hindus? Yet he did. All Yogi Adityanath is doing in reverting to the name Prayagraj is to atone for the Mughal-e-Azam's unforgivable sin.

Akbar was as much an invader after killing Hemu at the second battle of Panipat as Robert Clive was after vanquishing Siraj-ud-Daula at the battle of Plassey. The only difference was that Clive and his successors did not convert Hindus by force. Whereas, Akbar's successors did not hesiatate to deploy the sword to open the Hindu's option to reach *jannat*. For being more ruthless, the Indian governments have honoured them by naming some of central streets of Delhi after them and being reluctant to make any changes thereafter. Similarly, dozens of Indian cities and towns, not to speak of districts, honour the invaders.

On the other hand, what the successors of Clive named after themselves such as Curzon Road et al have been renamed. Even the spellings of some indigenous names have been proudly altered such as Cawnpore into Kanpur. Bombay has become Mumbai, Calcutta Kolkata and Madras Chennai, all British given local names. But Ahmedabad has not become Karnavati nor has Tughlaq given Daulatabad reverted to Devgiri. But India's first political party and once an institution of secularism now feels outraged because Allahabad is outstanding in shaping the country's modern political history.

Muslims have mysteriously escaped the stamp of an invader in Hindu eyes. They have stayed in India for a thousand years; and 70 years ago they took away a third of Hindustan and made it their homeland and called it Pakistan. On the other hand, the British ruled for 190 years, did not stay back, nor did they take away any territory. Yet, they carry the stigma of an invader. Hindus pat themselves on their backs for having waged a freedom struggle and sent back the British in 1947. Not a single street or city with a Muslim name, whether Tughlaq, Lodhi or Babar, has yet been replaced.

They exploited the land and its revenue to enjoy luxuries, run harems, acquire beautiful jewels and build forts and mausoleums. They hardly took any interest in promoting trade or industry and left no surplus for economic development. Due to their negligence, India missed the industrial revolution until after the British initiated modern mining, textile mills, and other manufacturing.

Obviously, they did so for profit but their ways of governance were such as to bring incidental benefits as well as modernisation to the country—be it the Railways, Post & Telegraph, the Laws, the Universities et al. Moreover, the curiousity of British officers and scholars led to the discovery of what was ancient Indian civilization which the Hindus themselves had largely forgotten. The Muslims destroyed more of the old especially temples, and created very little new except their own *mazhars*, *dargah* etc.

Agriculture was the main occupation of the people. However, Muslim rulers saw to it that the cultivators who were 99 percent Hindus, were left with no surplus. All kinds of taxes were used to extract as much state income as possible. The manner in which money was squeezed out of the cultivators was stated in a document of Feroz Tuglaq's time and quoted in Vol I of *The Cambridge Economic History of India, 1982*. It reads:

> A village was assigned to a trooper called Ziauddin, the sovereign having given him the right (haqq) over its poll tax (jiziya) and tax on cultivation (ziraat), so that he might spend the income on himself and his military equipment. The peasants, however, fled from the assigned village and settled in another village. Ziauddin insisted that the emigrants return to his village. It was his right to collect the poll tax from the peasants.

A charge often levelled against the British is that they divided the Indians, that is, they sowed the seeds of discord between Hindus and Muslims in order to rule India. Was this largely true? Even after the British crown assumed direct rule in 1858, no attempt was made to redivide the country. Uncannily, the Viceroy for the princely states and the Governor General for British India were combined in the same person.

Assuming that the British had adopted the policy of divide and rule, would they have taken the structural measures that they did early in their rule over India? For example, the three Presidencies of Bombay, Calcutta and Madras had been established independently of one another.

Yet, they were brought under one umbrella by the Regulating Act of 1773; thereafter Warren Hastings was promoted from Governor of Bengal to Governor General of India. Decades later, the Agra Presidency was formed, also to be answerable to theGovernor General.

If the policy was to divide, why was Lord Macaulay supported in his zeal for introducing English as the medium of instruction? This reform contributed more to bringing India together than any other. Without the English language how could a Bengali converse freely with a Gujarati? There was no *rashtra bhasha* or national language then. And without education in English, would our leaders across the subcontinent have imbibed from the West the spirit of liberty and the concept of nationalism?

The ruler could have taken steps, with the full support of the princely rulers to try to ensure that British India did not get easily integrated with the rest of the country. Instead, the Independence of India Act 1947, passed by Parliament in London, provided that every princely state must either join the Indian Union or the dominion of Pakistan.

The first gift of the English to India was the establishment of law and order across the country. Sir Percival Griffiths ICS, who served all his working life in India and wrote extensively, also deserves to be quoted. According to Sir Percival, on 6th July 1831, Raja Rammohan Roy said:

> Before the period in which India had become a tributary to Great Britain it was the scene of the most frequent and bloody conflicts. In the various provinces of the Dominion, nothing was to be seen but plunder and devastation; there was no security for property or for life, until, by the interference of this country, the great sources of discord were checked, education had advanced and the example of the British system of dominion had a conciliating effect on the natives of the East.

Mr Gopal Krishna Gokhale, complimenting the British, said that the the blessings of peace, the establishment of law and order, the introduction of Western education and the freedom of speech and appreciation of liberal institutions followed in their wake. After speaking of the anarchy and insecurity of the pre-British period, Dadabhai Naoroji went on to say, "Contrast this with the result of British rule. Law and order are its first blessings. Security of life and property is a recognised right of the people."

Enigma of Fascism

IN THE WAKE of the arrest of five 'urban naxals' by the Pune police, Rahul Gandhi has accused the BJP led government of being fascist. The writer doubts if he knows what fascism means although he is educated and certainly not an *anpadh gawar* to use Sanjay Nirupam's phrase. The expression fascist as a condemnation was first used frequently in Indira Gandhi's time. Her grandson is merely following the tradition set by her. Surely not many of the Congress leaders think that fascism is a synonym for despotism. The first is an ideology while the latter is brutal autocracy which was equally a feature of Stalinism exterminating the bourgeois and the kulaks, Nazism mass murdering Jews, as well as the white American settlers' treatment of the red Indians.

Fascism is class collaboration as communism is class conflict and capitalism is accused of class exploitation. Western Europe was deeply concerned by the Russian revolution of 1917 led by Vladimir Lenin and felt threatened. One of the reactions was the innovation of a new contrarian ideology, namely, of class collaboration in order to keep out class conflict taking over the society.

Some years ago, there was in the USA a celebration to commemorate Swami Vivekananda's birth century. That was an occasion when the secular fundamentalists were provoked to call the RSS and Vishwa Hindu Parishad fascist. A meeting presided over by the well known journalist, the late Kuldip Nayyar was held to dissuade the distinguished Ms Sonal Mansingh from going to Washington to present a dance item in connection with the celebration. In their view, their most decisive argument was that the organisers of the celebration were fascist. What they did not realise was that the word was not a political abuse that they thought it was. Benito Mussolini initiated the fascist movement in March 1919 at Milan and founded the party called Partito Nazional Fascista in November 1921. He ruled Italy for two decades. That is, however, too far-fetched to be abusive. Or, does the very word "fascist" denote political derogation? Perhaps it does to at least some members of the Indian intelligentsia. This is reason enough to recapitulate what was fascism.

The word "fascio" means a bundle or a bunch implying unity. To be effective the answer had to be something that would prove attractive to the peasants, to the workers, as well as to their unions. This was discovered in "class collaboration" as represented by fascism.

Prof Alfredo Rocco, the Minister of Justice in the Mussolini cabinet, set forth the gist of this new ideology in the course of a speech at Perugia in 1925. According to him, the society does not exist for the individual, but the individual for the society. Economic progress is a social interest and all classes of people should combine or collaborate to maximise production. The interests of the employers and the employed are after all identical. To ensure that this is practised, there must be a system of State discipline over class conflicts. Strikes and lockouts were alike illegal and punishable by heavy fine and in certain cases by imprisonment.

Wherever possible, the employers and workers in each industry, trade or profession were organised together in syndical association. Where it was not possible to form such syndicates, the unions and the employers' associations remained but combined to form guilds to coordinate and ensure cordiality. If collective bargaining could not end them satisfactorily, the disputes were referred to law courts assisted by experts. This is how class collaboration was conceptualised by the Fascist Party in Italy.

In practice, the economy was toned up by rearmament and public works. Soldiers were recruited in large numbers and so were workers in factories to produce arms. This would bring profits to the bourgeoisie who could then pay the proletariat well. Urban prosperity would increase demand for agricultural produce. What was left of the under-employed youth was absorbed by the armed forces. The promise to the whole nation was foreign conquests which would bring economic surpluses. The Albanian adventure and the invasion of Abyssinia were two efforts to fulfill this promise, until of course, World War II broke out.

Another example of the practice of fascism or class collaboration, albeit on a much more limited scale, was in Spain under Gen Francisco Franco. Neither the Italian nor the

Spanish experience is widely known in any great detail in India. What, however, the members of the intelligentsia are familiar with are the exploits of Adolf Hitler and his Nazi Party, whose full name was National Socialist German Workingmen's Party. It was founded by Hitler and his six comrades in Munich in 1920. The economic deprivation in Germany was much greater than witnessed in Italy. The country paid an exorbitant price for its defeat in World War I. The runaway inflation as well as the world depression ignited by the crash in share prices on the Wall Street in New York, in 1929, made matters unbearably hot for Germany. It was widely believed that the charismatic genius of Hitler and his programme of class collaboration, more or less, were on the lines of Mussolini's Italy, although on a far grander scale. They saved the country and its economy from utter collapse and a communist takeover.

Japan is another example of a fascist experiment. With the restoration of the Meiji regime in 1850 and the reforms initiated in 1868, were sown the seeds of ferment and economic progress. The gates of Japan opened and foreign contacts began with industrial development growing and the number of urban workers increased. By 1922, a Communist Party was founded. In the rural areas, silk farms sprang up and there was also fragmentation of farms; there grew discontent among the tenants who worked on them. Thereafter came the share market crash on Wall Street which triggered the Great Depression in 1929. The Japanese economy received its share of the tremors. One of the remedies to relieve the pains of the economic crisis was expansion through military conquest. The fact that the Japanese population had more than doubled since the Meiji restoration, more and more jobs were necessary. The ghost of Karl Marx and the scenes of the Russian Revolution were not invisible to the Japanese mind. War appeared to be a possible panacea which eventually led to the 1941 naval attack on Pearl Harbor, the American base of warships in the Pacific Ocean. This event was followed by the land invasion of British and French colonies in South-east Asia. Just before Pearl Harbor, Defence Minister Gen Tojo Hideki was made the Premier. The war moulded all classes of the Japanese people into one. This was an experiment of fascism in Asia.

So much for fascism and its smaller as well as grander variations. But what is its ugly connection with politics in India? India is not Europe. 2018 is not 1920. Communism is dead. There is some poverty but no financial collapse. Indian ethos has no record of imperialism and therefore no promise of foreign conquests would be credible. If an attempt is being made to compare the Jews of Germany and the Muslims of India, it is ridiculous. No one has accused the Muslims of betraying India, not even the BJP, whose only contention is that there has been appeasement of Muslim whims and pampering of the community's clergy. All in all, to call anyone a Fascist in India is to talk nonsense.

Much Ado about Babri Maqbarah

THE WRITER IS yet to come across a *masjid*, which is a place of prostration to Allah the merciful, which is named after any individual. On the other hand, a *dargah*, which is a tomb of a saint, is named after the holy man. So is a *mazhar* or a shrine of an important person named after him. There are many *maqbarahs* or places of graves that are generally constructed for rich and even ordinary persons merely to perpetuate their memory. Emperor Aurangzeb, commonly known as Alamgeer or Conqueror of the world, was humble enough before Allah to name his and his wife's grave "Biwi ka *Maqbarah*". He did not have the gumption to even call it a *mazhar* or a *dargah*, for that matter.

Similarly, it is difficult to think of a *masjid* without a minaret or several of them. As is well known, the function of a minaret is to enable a *muezzin* to stand as high as possible before he issues the *azaan*, or the call for worship. The higher he can stand, the greater the distance his voice or *baang* would carry and more would be the worshippers who would attend the prayer. In the days where there were no loudspeakers, the height of the minaret was crucial. An outstanding example of height is the *masjid* built by Aurangzeb on the banks of Ganga at Varanasi, which has two extremely tall minarets.

Another example is the big mosque at Istanbul, which was earlier a church of Hagia Sophia. The church was converted into a *masjid* by raising four minarets as tall as the pinnacle of the dome. In rural Anatolia and its wheatlands, most *masjid*s have a single minaret. But a minaret is there nevertheless. Or else the *baang* would not carry. When the writer visited Ayodhya, he had heard a great deal about the Babri *Masjid*, as if it was some historic piece of architecture. This was in early 1991. He was surprised at the uncomely sight of this enormous rough-looking trinity of domes. More surprising was the total absence of anything like a minaret. This made him suspicious enough to enquire, one by one, from three passing Muslim gentlemen, as to whether there were a *mehrab* or a *mimbar* inside, or a *wuzooh* for a wash before prayer. A few minutes earlier, he had been categorically told by a skull cap wearing gentleman that he could not go inside, hence the queries.

Whoever the writer talked to, including two shopkeepers, referred to it as the "Babri" *Masjid*. The writer had not earlier, or later come across a mosque named after any individual. His suspicion continued about the nature of the edifice in the absence of a minaret and the presence of the name Babri. On subsequent contemplation, he felt that perhaps the edifice was a *maqbarah* of Mir Baqi, one of the military commanders of

Babar in the latter's invasion of India. The date of the building has been consistently given as 1528 AD.

Babar won the First Battle of Panipat in April 1526. He and his men were new to India and generally busy establishing their rule based at Agra. How could Mir Baqi have had the opportunity to visit Ayodhya, have the Ram Temple demolished and had the huge Babri structure constructed, all in a matter of two years? In those days, five centuries ago, everything had to be done manually—breaking, building and all. It must have taken longer than two years. Babar died in 1530 while beseeching Allah the merciful to save the life of his ailing son Humayun.

Taking into account all these circumstances—the lack of a minaret, the presence of the name Babri, etc. is it possible that Mir Baqi did not forget the king he was beholden to, and he admired? He took his time to build this *maqbarah*, probably larger than any in India, as a compact building in loving memory of Zaheeruddin Mohammad Babar. In short, was the edifice Babri a *maqbarah* rather than a *masjid*? If so, why is the Sunni Personal Law Board making such a song and dance about the edifice and the land on which it stands? Up to a dozen *maqbarahs* were demolished under British rule in order to lay out the Delhi Golf Course.

Incidentally, Sir Arnold Toynbee had visited Delhi and Bombay in the 1950s to deliver the Azad Memorial Lectures. This was at the personal invitation of Jawaharlal Nehru. During the course of his lectures, Sir Arnold expressed surprise at having seen the *masjid* with tall minarets we have mentioned above, on the banks of the river Ganga, still standing. He went on to say that on his recent visit to Warsaw in Poland, he saw the cathedral in that city as a Roman Catholic edifice. When the Russians had conquered Warsaw a century or more ago, they had converted the earlier Catholic cathedral into a Russian orthodox church. The Poles could not tolerate this but were helpless. When they regained independence towards the end of WWI, they demolished the Russian church and rebuilt their own.

This pattern of behaviour was in evidence elsewhere too. Several wars were fought during the 1990s after the collapse of the Socialist Federal Republic of Yugoslavia (SFRY), particularly the 1991-1995 war in Croatia and Bosnia-Herzegovina. This was the biggest conflict in Europe since the Second World War, causing massive terror and brutality with approximately 150,000 deaths and several million people forcibly resettled. Although the Serbs, Croats, and Bosnian Muslims who fought this war were Europeans of Slavonic ancestry, they had significant and irreconcilable differences in religion. The Serbs are Eastern-Orthodox Christians, the Croats were Roman Catholics, and the Bosnian Muslims are Slavs Islamised after the Turkish conquest. The Serbs have always defended Christian Europe from invaders, most notably the Ottoman Turks. The heroic Serbian defence in the Battle of Kosovo against the Ottoman invaders in 1389 AD stands out as a landmark.

Conquering militias or armies in this 1992 inter-Yugoslav conflict destroyed the enemy's religious symbols and built their own to symbolically mark the territory. For example, the capital city of what is today called the "Serb Republic" of Bosnia and Herzegovina was ethnically cleansed of all its numerous historic and newer mosques, with the Serbs also expelling the local Muslims, ostensibly in retribution for centuries of Ottoman humiliation. Not only that, the Orthodox Serbs destroyed about 200 Catholic churches in Krajina in Croatia during their four year occupation of the town. This was Serb revenge on atrocities against the Orthodox Church by the Croat Nazi puppet state during WWII. The Catholic Croats had then murdered over a hundred Orthodox priests and three bishops, massacred about 1,000 Serbs in the town Glina and also razed its Orthodox Church of the Nativity.

Similar is the tale of Córdoba in Spain. It was originally a cathedral (Cathedral of Our Lady of the Assumption) but was conquered by the invading Moors and turned into a mosque in 784 AD by Abd-al-Rahman. It was reconquered by 1236 AD by King Ferdinand III of Castile during the Reconquista. The centre of the mosque was converted into a Catholic cathedral. The kings who followed added further Christian features.

More Muslim than Muslims

THOSE INTELLECTUALS, social activists or politicians who swear by secularism, appear to do better for the Muslims, as it were, than Muslim leaders themselves. They appear to want to do better for their neighbours than for their own children. They must believe that they are noble and, therefore, politically more than correct. People, especially believing Hindus, wonder whether these secularists understand what is secular, or know what the Muslims really need? Do they also equally care for the Christians?

This writer, in the course of discussions, had been told twice that the Haj subsidy or the finance deployed by the Indian government to facilitate Muslims to undertake the Haj pilgrimage should be gradually withdrawn. The late Syed Shahabuddin, a prominent leader of the Muslim community, was generally perceived as a militant advocate of its interests.

Yet, why should he have recommended the withdrawal of the subsidy? On checking up Islamic scriptures, it was discovered that Haj to Mecca and Medina should be undertaken only with one's own money. No money should be borrowed nor any subsidy taken from anyone if the pilgrim expects to enjoy divine blessings for being pious. Moreover, before embarking on the journey, the pilgrim should make sure that his trade or employment continues. His income should not be disturbed, nor should his family be troubled by shortage of money.

This writer was induced to petition the Supreme Court that the Haj subsidy should be abolished. In any case, India, according to the preamble of its Constitution is a secular state. Favouring members of one religion at the cost of the national exchequer is, therefore, unconstitutional. If, however, the government, regardless chose to persist with the subsidy, the petitioner should be exempted from the payment of income tax. After several hearings, on 28 January 2011, Justices Markandey Katju and Gyan Sudha Mishra delivered their judgment. If a small part of any tax is utilised for providing convenience to any religion that would not be violative of Article 27 of the Constitution, they wrote. Articles 14 and 15 are also not violated as there is no discrimination because governments also spend for other religions. Thus there was no force in this petition and it was dismissed. The Justices went on to add that in the face of the partition riots of 1947, the leadership of Jawaharlal Nehru kept a cool head. It was his greatness that he resisted the pressure to declare India a Hindu state, they added.

Ironically, a year later, Justices Aftab Alam and Rajana P Desai of the Supreme Court in the matter of Union of India vs Rafique Shaikh Bhikan, directed the Central government to progressively reduce the amount of subsidy and to completely eliminate it within a period of ten years from the date of the Judgment. They went on to add that Haj is a duty that mankind owes to Allah: "Those who can afford the expenses (for one's conveyance, provision and residence) should go". The government did not have to wait for ten years as directed by the apex court but was able to eliminate the Haj subsidy by 2018.

How right Syed Shahabuddin was! Does this not show that Hindu secularists, including the advocates of Nehruvian secularism do not understand the Muslim faith? Islamic scriptures, by implication, permit the desecration of any place of worship that contains idols, whether a temple or a church. Hindu temples necessarily have statues of *avatars* and deities, which amounts to *butparasti* or idolatry, which is forbidden in Islam. So too are the statues of Virgin Mary in a church or that of Jesus Christ on a crucifix. This explains why thousands of Hindu, Buddhist and Jain temples were desecrated in India; the fate of churches has gone backwards and forwards between Muslims and Christians in Europe. A subsidiary motivation would be to abolish a competing religion from attracting converts. However, the very same Islamic scriptures forbid *momins* (the faithful) from worshiping at a place desecrated by the zealots of their own faith. By the same token, the thousands of temples that have been desecrated or converted/recycled into mosques must not be attended. Yet, when this issue is raised, the secularists argue that one cannot carry the past on one's sleeve. Let bygones be bygones; revivalism is the enemy of progress.

As Janab Wasim Rizvi (Shia Waqf Board chief) has proposed, *madrasah* should be wound up. His observation was that they help to produce some young men with the inclination to join terrorism. It is possible that Rizvi knows that the type and level of education in many of these *madrasas* is obsolete and too limited for the current competitive world. The present demands an advanced level of education if one is to obtain secular employment beyond the level of class 4. Otherwise, the only alternative future for such students would be some level of priesthood. But Rizvi's is a Muslim voice; why is it that not a single secularist whose heart bleeds for Muslim welfare says anything? Why not appeal to the maulanas to borrow a few pages from the *Ahl-e-Kitab* (People of the Book) Christians, many of whom dedicate their lifetimes to teaching and more teaching? Nor are secularists asking *madrasas* to enlist themselves in the Madhyamik boards if not also CBSE or ICSE.

Strictly speaking, a secularist is one who believes in separating all religion from the state or government. As the US Constitution says, a wall should be built between religion and the state. The concept of secularism was born with the Reformation in 16th century Europe. It, however, took time to crystallise but eventually made nationalism replace religion as the ideological basis of many countries in Europe. Karl Marx and his followers took this concept to the extreme by decrying religion as the opium of the masses. The Marxists said there was no God and declared themselves atheists. When the Soviet Union replaced the Tsarist Empire, churches, mosques and synagogues were converted into offices, departmental stores and put to such other civic uses.

Secularism, as understood in India, is called *Sarva Dharma Samabhav* meaning all religions together from a family. Nehruvian secularism has distorted it into favouring only Muslims, and not worrying about the rest. Most sensible Muslims would like to be treated as equals and not be a favoured lot, lest they arouse Hindu resentment. But, as we have seen above, India's secularists seldom worry about what precisely Muslims want.

In India, Hinduism itself is tantamount to secularism for the simple reason that this faith has not dabbled in the State. Hinduism is not a political religion but only the pursuit of spiritual thought, worship and festivals, unlike Islam, which is a comprehensive prescription for all aspects of life. Christianity, as per the old Testament, meant Caesar and the Church to have their respective spheres. Nevertheless, the Bishops and Cardinals in Europe did have their say in government. Up to the 18th century, France had three houses in its National Assembly, the Lords, the Bishops and the Commons. Moreover, the faith provided the ideological basis until after the Reformation began inspiring nationalism.

For long centuries, Hinduism faced no adversaries or even competition. Whoever came from outside or was already around joined their way of life. If the new group wished to maintain its distinct identity, it formed a separate caste but the central beliefs remained the same. It was only with the advent of Islam into India that tension and conflicts began. And, for yet more centuries, the Hindus did not comprehend what a compact, aggressive religion meant. Conversion was a new phenomenon. Understanding Islam through a Hindu mindset was to confuse oneself. To this day, there are many Hindus who feel that resisting Islamic inroads in an organised way is to Islamise Hinduism. Secularism is an expression redundant in India. Toleration or lack of it are relevant.

Secularise Aligarh University

THAT STUDENTS AT a university should provoke the police into filing criminal complaints is shameful. Aligarh University has a long history of students with doubtful loyalty to the country. Qaid-e-Azam Jinnah had lavished praises on the institution calling it the "arsenal of Pakistan". One reference is Yuvraj Krishan's book *Understanding Partition.* "MA Jinnah justifiably and aptly described the Aligarh Muslim University (AMU) as the arsenal of Pakistan. AMU's teachers and students actively supported the Pakistan movement and mobilised support for the policies and programmes of the Muslim League for the division of India and creation of the Muslim-majority state of Pakistan. Granting special status to AMU has regenerated the pre-independence brain trust of the Pakistan movement. A secular state has established an anti-secular institution." *Understanding Partition: India Sundered, Muslims Fragmented* by Yuvraj Krishan; published Mumbai, 2002.

A sizeable number of its students had gone all the way to Punjab to campaign for the Muslim League during the 1945-46 elections to the Constituency Assembly. When some of the voters asked the students what was there for them in the results, since UP could not be a part of Pakistan, their reply was that they had come to make sure the outcome brings a New Medina. The students had issued a manifesto which declared that "Pakistan is our Deliverance, Defence and Destiny. We deny that we are one nation with the Hindus and the rest".

Sir Syed Ahmad Khan, the founder of the Mohammadan Anglo Oriental College (MAO), Aligarh, was a witness to the 1857 happenings. From 1858 right up to 1898, Syed Ahmad Khan was the pivot around whom the Muslim politics moved. In his speeches made at Lucknow and Meerut on 28th December 1887, and 16th March 1888, respectively, he laid down the fundamental guidelines for Muslims to follow in their interaction with the British and the Congress Party. He asked Muslims not to join the Congress Party and support only the British.

This policy decided once for all the attitude of the whole Muslim community towards the Congress. Few Muslims of note since then have joined the Congress except one or two. During his lifetime, Syed Ahmad did not make any departure from his political creed.

The late Sir Aga Khan who had led the Muslim delegation to Viceroy Minto in 1906 and demanded separate electorate, also complimented the university for playing a vital role in the creation of Pakistan. In his autobiography published in 1954 he has written:

> Often, in a civilized history, a university has supplied the springboard for a nation's intellectuals and spiritual renaissance ... Aligarh is no exception to this rule. But we may claim with pride that Aligarh was the product of our own efforts and of no outside benevolence and surely it may also be deemed that the independent, sovereign nature of Pakistan was born in the Muslim University of Aligarh.

Another Muslim leader, Zia-ul-Hasan Faruqui described Aligarh as the training centre of the Mujahideen-e-Pakistan. Muslim leaders like Maulana Azad and Humayun Kabir were vilified and physically abused by the students of AMU in 1942. In 1946, communal riots took place in Aligarh. Four persons were killed and property worth lakhs was destroyed. An enquiry conducted by the Divisional Commissioner John Stone found that apart from the city Muslims, students of AMU had started the riots. In October 1947, the Pakistan Government was found to be recruiting officers for the Pakistan army from Aligarh Muslim University. GB Pant, the then Chief Minister of UP had to direct the Vice Chancellor of AMU not to allow Pakistani officers to visit the university.

The Aligarh Movement: This was launched by Syed Ahmad Khan in the 1860s. In terms of its significance and consequences for India, this was the most important movement launched by the Muslims in modern history. The movement has been called "The Aligarh Movement" because its headquarters were at Aligarh. Prof MS Jain in his research monograph *The Aligarh Movement (1965)* asks: Why did we not develop into a homogeneous nation and why did the Muslims of India, generally speaking, chalk out a path different from that of the other communities in India? The movement of Muslim regeneration initiated by Sir Syed Ahmad Khan, provides the answer.

Richard Symonds who came out with his book *The Making of Pakistan* in 1949 on the morrow of the emergence of Pakistan has written: In politics, he (Syed Ahmad Khan) had stated that Muslims were a nation who could not and must not be submerged in a system of government by majority vote. The Pakistanis rightly claim him as one of the fathers of their country.

In the *Aligarh Institute Gazette* of 22 Sept 1893, Sir Syed wrote: "Mahomedans may accept English supremacy because they have been conquered by Englishmen, but who is to make them submit to the supremacy of the Hindus, whom for 700 years they regarded their slaves." Sir Syed laid down as a matter of policy for the Muslims—undiluted loyalty to the British regime; no truck with the Indian National Congress; and pursuit of modern education.

Prof Wilfred Smith, who had taught at Lahore for years, has said that by 1941 Aligarh had become the emotional centre of Pakistan, whereas Sir Aga Khan claims that the independent, sovereign nation of Pakistan was born in the Muslim University of Aligarh.

UP Muslims were at the heart of Muslim separatism, wrote Prof Francis Robinson of Holloway College, London. They founded and, with the exception of the Bombay-based Jinnah, mainly led the organisations which represented the Muslim interest in Indian politics. Syed Ahmed Khan, founder of the Muhammadan Anglo Oriental College at Aligarh, directed quite early the Muslim political activity and nurtured many Muslim League politicians. He followed this with the establishment of the All India Muslim Educational Conference in 1886, which helped him impress his political will on Indian Muslims. In 1906, large numbers of Muslims from UP flocked to Dacca to found the All India Muslim League. In this organisation the secretaryship was the most powerful position, and between 1906 and 1910 it was held by UP Muslims in Aligarh. After World War I, Muslims from the same province set up an association of Indian ulema and made the Central Khilafat Committee an organisation of all India importance.

Soon after his appointment as Vice-Chancellor, Ali Yavar Jung suggested certain changes in the rules of admission. Making this a pretext an agitation was almost immediately set afoot by those who were opposed to him. Once started, the agitation did not remain peaceful. As a matter of fact, it ended up in an attempt to assassinate the Vice-Chancellor to the horror of everyone. The students marched with a coffin to the office where the Vice-Chancellor was holding a meeting of the Court, broke into the meeting hall and assaulted him so seriously that no one could have doubts that the intention was to kill him. They nearly succeeded in their nefarious mission.

Ali Yavar Jung, however, had a miraculous escape. Justice MC Chagla was satisfied that the students alone were not responsible for this heinous plot. There were others hiding in the background. Some members of the Court obviously sympathised with the students, and instead of going to the rescue of the Vice-Chancellor, they looked the other way. He thought drastic measures were called for, as it was impossible for the Vice-Chancellor to function in the existing set-up of the university. Chagla, therefore, got the central cabinet's approval to the promulgation of an ordinance by which the existing Executive Council and the Court were dissolved and the government was empowered to set up a nominated Executive Council and Court. Chagla took pains to see that the persons nominated were sympathetic to the Vice-Chancellor, and held similar views with regard to the policy to be adopted in running the university.

A raging and tearing campaign was started in the country by fanatical elements everywhere. Chagla was charged with being a dictator and interfering with the rights of autonomy of the university. The demand was made that the administration should be left to the Muslim community which had a unique interest in its well-being and that the ordinance should be revoked. Justice Chagla reminded the agitators firmly that the Aligarh University was not a minority institution as defined in the Constitution; that it was neither established nor maintained by the Muslim community; that it was a national institution in which the whole nation was interested and that, though undoubtedly it had a special purpose to serve, namely, the advance of Arabic and Islamic studies, that did not change its essential character because even non-Muslims might have an interest in such studies. He said, "If some students wish to leave the university, as they have threatened to, let them go. Without them Aligarh should be better for the studies of the rest."

Govind Dev Temple in Vrindavan

THE DESECRATION OF the Govind Dev Temple at Vrindavan is unique; it was neither complete nor was it converted into a mosque. It was cut into half vertically. Whenever Aurangzeb happened to be in Delhi or Agra, at night he would see a *mashaal* or torch lighting the sky. How can any light shine higher than mine in my capital? It must be put off once and for all, felt the Mughal. By 1669, he lost his patience, sent his men and had the Govind Dev Temple cut in half, four storeys reduced to two. On the truncated roof he had a *mehrab* erected so that he could pray on his visits.

Probably no other desecrated temple had been the subject of so much repair and refurbishment by British rulers. Of supreme importance was the fact of the *mandir* being restituted to Hindu devotees. It was the greatest act of *Shuddhi* or purification although performed before Swami Dayanand Saraswati reintroduced Vedic procedures. FS Growse, the Magistrate of Mathura district in the 1870s, therefore deserves a place in the hall of Hinduism. The Govind Dev Temple at Vrindavan, Mathura, is indeed massive; its plinth is 105 feet by 117 feet. It is estimated that the original height was about 110 feet without which it would not have been possible to see the *mashaal* or torch either from Agra or from Delhi. The temple was built in 1590 AD by Maharaja Mansingh of Jaipur

The Govind Dev Temple is also unique for several other reasons but we shall come to these a little later. For the satisfaction of its desecrators, the sanctum sanctorum was destroyed. Fortunately, the idol of Sri Krishna or Govind had been removed to Jaipur by the *pujaris* in anticipation of Aurangzeb's proposed visit in 1670 AD; the emperor was already notorious as an iconoclast. The roof of the truncated edifice was to be reserved for *namaz*. No sooner had the *mehrab* been constructed, as illustrated in the photograph in *History of Indian and Eastern Architecture* by James Fergusson, Aurangzeb inaugurated it himself by offering prayers.

All except two statuettes were defaced, including the one at the door of what is now the temple, after crossing the foyer hall. The destruction was not confined to the upper floors. It extended to the hundreds of statuettes that even today adorn the temple walls outside as well as inside, the ceilings and doors. The iconoclast overlooked two small statuettes, one of Sri Krishna and the other of Radha, on the outside of the left part as one faces the temple.

An American historian of Indian architecture, George Mitchell, has concluded that the original sanctum sanctorum was destroyed. In his own words, "Once the *garbhagriha* had been torn down, there was little point in further wreckage... It seems to me that only those with some understanding of the ritual significance of the *garbhagriha* would have been capable of desecrating a temple in this careful manner."

Prof R Nath introduces the subject of the Govind Dev Temple by quoting Aurangzeb's decree of April 1669. It said, "Eager to establish Islam, Aurangzeb issued orders to the governors of all the provinces to demolish the schools and temples of the infidels and with the utmost urgency put down the teaching and the public practice of the religion of these disbelivers". The great temple of Govind Dev fell a victim to iconoclastic vandalism within a year of the decree. Its inner sanctum and its superstructure were almost entirely destroyed. The main hall was also damaged. Sculpted figures on the *dvarasakha* were literally defaced.

The temple has yet another unique feature. According to an article in the *Calcutta Review* quoted by Growse:

> Aurangzeb had often remarked about a very bright light shining in the far distant south east horizon, and in reply to his enquiries regarding it, was told that it was a light burning in a temple of great wealth and magnificence at Vrindavan. He accordingly resolved that it should be put out and soon after sent some troops to the place who plundered and threw down as much of the temple as they could and then erected on the top of the ruins a mosque wall where, in order to complete the desecration, the emperor is said to have offered up his prayers.

Incidentally, the canopy standing on four pillars, which must have acted as a shed for the burning torch or *mashaal*, is lying on the ground at the back of the present sanctum sanctorum. It was so fixed, presumably in the 1870s. It has no relevance to the temple's architecture. This reinforces the belief that this canopy belonged to the top of the once towering temple.

While Aurangzeb's ego might have been gratified, the desecration took with it what is described by Fergusson as one of the most elegant temples in India, and the only one perhaps, from which a European architect might borrow a few things. Growse added that, "It is not a little strange that of all the architects who have described this famous building, not one has noticed its most characteristic feature—the harmonious combination of dome and spire—which is still quoted as the great crux of modern art, though nearly 300 years ago the difficulty was solved by the Hindus with characteristic grace and ingenuity". I should myself have thought that 'solemn' or 'imposing' was a more appropriate term than 'elegant' for so massive a building, and that the suggestions that might be derived from its study were 'many' rather than 'few'; but the criticism is in intention a complimentary one.

A nineteenth century architect Henry Hardy Cole, who had toured India widely, wrote: "I am not sure that the restoration of the uppermost parapet is correct and think that it would have been better to leave the superstructure as it appeared when I first saw it, with all the evidence of Aurangzeb's destructive hand".

A number of motives have been attributed to the invaders who desecrated temples, such as looting of treasures, subduing the populace by arousing dread, informing the area that a sultan had replaced the raja. There is, however, no other instance of a temple being desecrated because it defied the ego of an emperor.

Justice Sen on the Hindu State

JUSTICE SR SEN of Meghalaya High Court said on December 13, 2018 that India should have been declared a Hindu country after Pakistan broke away to become a Muslim country. For example, until the 1789 revolution, France had three houses of its National Assembly, one comprising Abbots and Bishops. To go secular, the country had to abolish this third house. What is Caeser's (the ruler's) should be given to him and what is God's should be His. In other words, the 16th century Reformation which became the springboard of secularism or the separation of the Church from the State was, in a way, sanctioned by the Bible. It was, therefore, not difficult to ease out the clergy from the running of the government. On the other hand, in an Islamic State, the sovereignty belongs to Allah and not the people. Whatever sweet secular things Jinnah might have said on 11 August 1947 to the Constituent Assembly, the first Constitution of Pakistan attributes sovereignty to Allah.

Let us for a few moments keep aside what Macaulay or English education taught us and consider what the Hindu thinkers thought of their state. The *rajya* or state comprised the monarch whose minimal duties were threefold. He had to defend the borders of the kingdom's territory, to protect the lives and property of his subjects and to appoint a competent *yuvaraj* or successor; not necessarily his son. King Bharat, the forefather of the Kurus had seven sons but he overlooked all of them for not being sufficiently competent. He anointed Bhumanyu who justified his choice. If the monarch wished to go beyond these three duties, it was at his discretion.

The Vedic ethos was current at the time and the elite followed the Sanatan Dharma or the eternal faith whose cornerstone was *karma* leading to *bhagya* which was the factor of cause and effect. There was no concept of religion and its hierarchies as for example in Christianity. When Lord Mahavira projected his philosophy called Jainism, it caused no problem. It so happened that when Emperor Chandragupta Maurya decided to retire, he became a Jain sadhu and spent the rest of his life around Shravanbelagola in today's Karnataka. There was tolerance of this different viewpoint of how to lead life.

Emperor Ashoka's espousal of Budhism as his faith and its wherewithals of an organised religion did lead to tensions. Especially so, when he took a lead in preaching Buddhism; for example, he sent his daughter Sanghamitra and his son Mahendra to Sri Lanka. They and their order converted a large section of the people to Buddhism, people who are now known as Sinhalas. Ashoka sent his missions to many places including Tibet and Asian lands east of India. A monarch turning a proselytizer was against the Hindu way and evoked resistance. The one great saint who led the opposition was Adi Shankaracharya in the eighth century. In European terms this was the first clash between Hinduism or Indic toleration. The India of those times could not digest a mix up of governance and preaching a religion.

When Islam first came to India, it was confined to Sindh where Muhammad-bin-Qasim won some territory, built a few mosques and converted some people. Nevertheless, it seemed like an episode in isolation, especially in those days when communications were scanty. Mahmud of Ghazni's attack, three centuries later, appeared like the adventures of a marauder who was also barbaric. He did butcher people, *pujaris* and destroyed temples but his thrust appeared like that of a powerful robber.

An ongoing trauma settled on the Hindus on the morrow of Muhammad Ghori's conquest of Delhi and his appointment of Qutb-ud-din Aibak to rule from Delhi. With the government authority in the grip of the sultanate, the Hindus, unaccustomed to such brutality, failed to produce an answer. Yes, Maharana Pratap did defend Mewar successfully while Chhatrapati Shivaji demonstrated how Hindus could avenge some of their defeats. As did Maharajah Ranjit Singh teach stern lessons to the invaders. But these were three oases in a desert of some 551 years. Even this long desert was interrupted by the East India Company and Robert Clive at the Battle of Plassey in 1757, whereafter Bengal, Bihar and Odisha fell to the British. Hindus had the vicarious satisfaction of seeing the Muslim ruling class tumbling from their thrones and sitting on the floor. However, it was not a Muslim defeat at Hindu hands.

There is a philosophical block which comes in the way of the Hindu being a ready killer and fighter. He grows up believing that his salvation lies in his self actualisation through his personal *karma;* whereas his Muslim counterpart grows up watching animals' throats being cut as the *kalima* is read to make his meat *halal* or permissible. Moreover, as a man he is made to believe that his salvation lies in his serving his society, ideally through getting killed in a jihad for the sake of his society. A *shaheed* or such a martyr goes immediately to heaven without waiting years for *qayamat* or doomsday.

The Hindu, on the other hand, is told that all living beings are members of his family. So when he kills, he is participating in a homicide of his relative, however distant. In his book *Thoughts on Pakistan* published in 1941, Dr BR Ambedkar endorses MA Jinnah's proposal for Partition of undivided India. His main argument was that it was better to have the enemy outside one's borders than inside. Without being more explicit it was obvious that the two cultures were not naturally congenial and both would be better off living in separate countries. Jinnah and seven of his leading Muslim League colleagues had wanted an exchange of populations. They desired Muslims to gather in Pakistan by migrating. Similarly, non-Muslims should vacate the territory of Pakistan.

As distinct from Europe and America, the East has no native concept of the 'secular'. Whether Arabic, Persian or Urdu, there is no synonym for the word secular. Islam is an all embracing prescription for life, whether individual or collective, social or political, religious or otherwise. The question of separating any of them does not arise. In contrast, Christianity provided in the Bible itself that there was no need of separating anything from the State. It has no concept of the secular. One synonym for Hinduism is tolerance and another would, in the current context, be secularism. In fact, until Prime Minister Indira

Gandhi thrust it during the 1976 Emergency, there was no mention of secularism in our Constitution. The crux of what Justice Sen has asked for is a Hindu, and therefore a tolerant State.

ISLAMISATION OF EUROPE

Time Stands for Merkel, not for the World

ON 16TH DECEMBER 2018, German Chancellor Angela Merkel was reported to have stated at Davos that the New World Order based on globalism is being destroyed by President Donald Trump. She did not approve of the US President's message of "polarization, protectionism and populism". She poured scorn on the popular patriotic movement currently sweeping across Europe, USA, Australia, Brazil and other parts of the world.

Evidently, Frau Angela Merkel is living in the past and is not in step with the times. If she were a student of history, she would realise that with the fall of the Berlin Wall in her own country, the demise of communism and the breakup of the Soviet Union, a new chapter in world history had opened. The world had sighed with relief that the Cold War or World War

III had ended and the Damocles' sword of a nuclear blowup had retreated into its scabbard. The world had tired of the butchery and destruction witnessed in World War II, which had spread right across the Eurasian landmass, without leaving out even fringes of Africa. Not long before this ghastly phase, the killing of 50 million people had taken place in the first War, which again had witnessed senseless carnage. Imagine the civilizational fatigue that had been witnessed in a matter of 31 years.

In their wisdom, world leaders stepped out to abolish, even if gradually, nationalism, which they perceived as the cause of these ugliest three decades in history. They banked on the United Nations Organisation to be a shadow of a global confederation, a world order, a platform wherefrom nations could speak but do little to stop the fighting. This was the New World Order dreamt of by the idealists, which Angela Merkel spoke about at Davos. The dream, however, lasted only as long as the statesmen slept. They woke up to find two big blocs, one led by the USA and the other by the Soviet Union, manufacturing nuclear weapons. Although they were allies in the second War, so began the Cold War or World War III.

Another name for it was the balance of terror. The atomic bombs dropped on Hiroshima and Nagasaki had taught the combatants what nuclear weapons meant and hence no bomb was burst during the new war. However, the Soviet bloc known as the Second World lost more than could be imagined. The USA and its allies, called the First World, won hands down. This happened in 1991 and yet another new chapter in history was opened.

Angela Merkel was the leader who was born with this chapter and continues to loyally stick by it. She did not realise that what Prof Samuel Huntington predicted in terms of the clash of civilizations, had commenced at Munich in her own country in the 1972 Olympic Games when a dozen Israeli athletes were massacred by West Asian terrorists. Although realised much later, this was the beginning of a clash between Islamists and virtually the rest of the world. At least five of the six continents have been involved. With the election of Jair Bolsonaro as the President of Brazil, it is apprehended that the clash may have touched the shores of even the sixth continent, namely, Latin America.

Regardless of these developments, it should have been clear soon after the breakup of the Soviet Union that the North Atlantic Treaty Organization (NATO) had become redundant: whom was this organization against? It was established in 1949 as the first ring around communist Russia in defence of the Free World in general and Western Europe in particular. The second part of the ring was the Baghdad Pact, which became the Central Treaty Organization (CENTO). The third was the South East Asia Treaty Organization (SEATO). The last two treaties were wound up in due course, but the first still survives at an enormous expenditure, with the USA paying most of it. Being across the Atlantic Ocean, America faced the least danger and yet paid the most. President Donald Trump has raised this question twenty-five years after it could have been. Yet, Frau Merkel labels this questioning as 'destabilization'.

The lady could not understand that the Islamists are on a warpath. She could not anticipate that more and more Muslim migrants would be arriving in Western Europe. Some kind of a defensive arrangement, call it a wall or otherwise—should have been made around the European Union. It was not difficult to anticipate that the offensive by the ISIS in Iraq and Syria would cause an exodus from these countries. Instead, Frau

Merkel prepared herself to welcome the Syrian migrants into Germany. Moreover, along with France, Berlin worked out how many migrants each EU country should be prepared to host. Not unexpectedly, a number of EU members protested. Poland, Hungary, Austria, Spain and later Italy put their foot down and said a big NO to immigration. Now, Frau Merkel has realised her folly and has offered each migrant 3,000 euros as a return package. Notwithstanding, she has the audacity to question President Trump and his building the wall against Mexican migrants rushing into the USA.

Instead of helplessly watching North Korea brandishing its nuclear potential, President Trump intervened with the ultimate hope of inducing this Chinese satellite to disarm. In the bargain, one could allege that he has interfered with the Chinese backyard. He has reopened the issue of US-China trade relations as the former found it to be disadvantageous. Consequently, the various commitments which had been made on the platform of the World Trade Organization (WTO) may need revision. Not every effect of the agreement could be envisaged by every country and amendments became necessary. A conservative observer would criticise an upward revision of import-export tariffs as going back on one's word whereas Donald Trump would see it as serving his country's best interests.

Even when former President Barak Hussein Obama had a nuclear agreement signed between the USA and Iran, there were sceptics who suspected that the latter's intentions were to go nuclear militarily. They were not entirely in favour of having nuclear fuel for peaceful uses. President Trump was one of the sceptics. As a result, he reopened the agreement which met with Iranian disapproval. Hence the sanctions on its trade were reimposed.

Coming to Judea, the Trump administration saw greater advantage in getting closer to Israel than merely being politically correct. The President, therefore, recognised Jerusalem as the capital of Israel and transferred the USA embassy there from Tel Aviv. When the ancient city was divided with Palestine, the latter was the capital. No other country protested but some European leaders might have seen the change as pro-semetic and not fair to Palestine. Frau Merkel is clearly a conservative and, to that extent, not in step with time as seen in her treatment of the Syrian migrants. Not everyone realises that there is no present except for some fleeting seconds. One can, therefore, mentally live either in the past or alternatively in the future. The German Chancellor appears to belong to the former category, whereas Donald Trump wants to catch up on time. "For the first time, an American President believes that Europe is a has-been," in the words of Bruno Macães, a senior fellow at the Hudson Institute, trying to explain the Trump doctrine. Briefly, Trump's approach to Europe is this: he will not allow the United States to be dragged down with Europe, even if that means bringing about a new schism in the trans-Atlantic alliance.

Europe and Christo-Muslim Conflict

FOR QUITE A while now, some citizens have been complaining that the environment in India is afflicted by insecurity. More recently, voices are being raised of institutions being overturned. It is, however, not realised that the flow of history itself is undergoing a churning. Certainly since the Berlin Wall fell in 1989. In order to understand this elementary truth, it is useful to know that a Christo-Muslim conflict began in Europe only a year after Mohammad bin Qasim invaded Sind in 711 AD. The conflict continued in less or more intensity, and is the most prominent problem in the great continent today.

In a recent talk with the BBC, Witold Waszczykowski, Poland's former Foreign Minister (2015-18) emphasised that his country wants a democracy, but "a democracy without adjectives". The government wants to be left free to pursue its people's interests. For instance, Poland has assigned 17 lakh visas to enable immigration from Ukraine and Belarus. However, Waszczykowski is emphatic that adherence to EU immigration norms and other rules does not mandate Poland to let in Syrians and North Africans and allowing them to settle in his country. He has explicitly spoken out against the mix up of Christians and Muslims.

This aversion to what Waszczykowski calls a "mix up" is not based merely on recent events, but on Europe's experience of Christo-Muslim conflicts beginning 712 AD. Incidentally, Mohammad bin Qasim, the first Islamic invader to conquer territory in India, reached Sind the previous year, namely 711 AD.

Christo-Muslim clashes in Europe commenced with the Moor invasion of the Iberian Peninsula from North Africa, capturing most of it, crossing the Pyrenees and entering France. The Moors reached Poitiers in central France where they were defeated by Charles Martel by 732 AD and turned back, never to return. The Moors, however, ruled Spain and Portugal for centuries till their expulsion by resurgent Christians; Granada was the last outpost which they left in 1492. The erstwhile invaders had to bear their share of revenge. The victorious Christian retaliators placed three alternatives before them; reconversion to Christianity, leaving Iberia immediately, or death. Most chose the first of the conditions and came to be known as Moriscos.

The second long Christo-Muslim war were the eight Crusades. The first was fought in 1095 AD, while the last was in 1291. Christians strove to recover their holy lands, especially Jerusalem, lost to Arabs in 638 AD. The Arabs allowed Christians to visit the holy city freely for over four centuries, but the Turks, who captured Palestine by 1071, ended this privilege. European reaction to this Turkish arbitrariness was the first Crusade. By July 1099, Crusaders from Western Europe had captured Jerusalem which remained with them until Saladin, the great Turkish sultan, snatched it back in 1187. Christian zeal for the holy land sustained but by the end of the last Crusade, nothing much had been achieved. Christians had effectively lost the long war. Jerusalem's Muslim rulers, however, allowed a few Christians to stay on as caretakers of their holy places, but they were not permitted to preach.

Fear of a Muslim takeover of Christian Europe has not vanished; on the contrary, it has only intensified in the light of recent happenings. Poland isn't alone in bluntly voicing its opposition to Muslim migration. In its parliamentary elections in April this year, Hungary's ruling party Fidesz's campaign concentrated on a single issue—no immigrants. Not that Hungary was being overrun by immigrants; it has one of the lowest foreign born populations in the developed world. Its own fertility rates are below even the European average. But the Hungarian election campaign was not a response to any demographic development. It is a cultural crusade that has made Hungary the least refugee friendly country in Europe.

Hungary is not inherently anti-immigrant. In 2016, (official data is available till then) 23,803 foreigners moved there; numbers have been stable since before Prime Minister Viktor Orban came to power in 2010. Interestingly, fewer than half of the migrants were EU citizens. So it isn't immigration per se that Hungary has a problem with. Orban's Hungary is fiercely against a certain kind of immigrant.

Blunter assertion comes from government spokesman Zoltan Kovacs, "We've been living next to Islam and with Islam for 500 years. We know it's not going to integrate. We treat it as a "civilizational problem". He further said that Muslim immigrants create "parallel societies" in the European countries that receive them—the Hungarians want none of that. A 2016 Pew Research study revealed 72 percent of Hungarians have negative views of Muslims in their country, far higher than the EU average of 43 percent.

From the Moorish conquest of Spain (712 AD) to the second Turkish siege of Vienna (1683), Europe was under constant threat from Islam. All but the easternmost provinces of the Islamic realm had been taken from Christian rulers, and the vast majority of the first Muslims, west of Iran and Arabia, were converts from Christianity. North Africa, Egypt, Syria, even Persian-ruled Iraq had been Christian, where their religion was older and more deeply rooted than in most of Europe. Their loss was sorely felt and heightened the fear that a similar fate awaited Europe. The fall of Constantinople, known as the Rome of the East and the seat of the Byzantine Empire and Eastern Christianity to the invading Turks in 1453 is, to this day, regarded as the greatest tragedy to have befallen Christendom. The Turkish Caliphate ended in 1924 following the Ottoman Empire's defeat and collapse after World War I. Today's Turkey, under its neo-Ottomanesque ruler Erdogan, who does not disguise his pan-Islamist ambitions, only further exacerbates fears among Europeans, the assertions of the EU 'elites' to the contrary notwithstanding.

Many European writers, litterateurs and intellectuals warn that in the years to come, "the possibility that Europe will become a museum or a cultural amusement is real". The late historian Walter Laqueur offered a far-sighted prognosis about Europe's crisis. He was one of the first to understand that the current crisis isn't about economics. Because of low birth rates,

Europe is dramatically shrinking. If current trends continue, Laqueur said, a hundred years from now Europe's population "will be only a fraction of what it is today, and in two hundred years, some countries may have disappeared".

This spectre is becoming more visible and frequently discussed by writers. French writer Michel Houellebecq through his best-selling novels, such as *Submission*, has often lamented that "the Western world as a whole is committing suicide". French President Emmanuel Macron, known to wear his liberalism on his sleeve, while referring to France-bound migration from North Africa in 2017 had called Africa's problems "civilizational". The unspoken part is that this African influx with burgeoning fertility rates is Muslim.

More worrying is Europe's loss of confidence in its hard-won Enlightenment values, such as personal freedoms, reason and science ousting superstition, and the separation of church and state. These are very important if Europe truly wishes to survive. Distinguished American historian Victor Davis Hanson recently wrote:

> Judged by the great historical determinants of civilizational power—fuel, energy, education, demography, political stability, and military power—Europe is waning. It spends a mere 1.4% of its collective GDP on defence. And with a fertility rate of less than 1.6%, Europe is slowly shrinking and ageing—hence the short-sighted immigration policy of Angela Merkel who apparently sees immigration also as a solution to the demography crisis and a shortcut to low-cost labour.

Some European Union politicians have advocated having more children as the answer to Europe's demographic problems in the looming conflict with Muslims. Italy's interior minister Matteo Salvini who heads the anti-immigration League Party, has said that his country's and Europe's youth ought to have more children rather than bring in modern-day slaves (i.e. African and other migrants) to "replace the children Europeans are not having".

Hungarian Prime Minister Viktor Orbán has called on Europeans to stop the "demographic decline" by investing more in traditional families. Catholic bishop Andrew Nkea Fuanya of Mamfe, Cameroon, recently said about low birth rates in Europe: "With the backdrop of the Islamic invasion, if you look through history, where the Church slept and was diverted from the Gospel, Islam took the advantage and came in. This is what we are seeing in Europe; the Church is sleeping, and Islam is creeping in... Europe is being Islamised".

Europeans have begun to realise that an ageing and tired Europe is not a partisan or electoral issue; it is a civilizational one. This issue will also decide the future of the European Union, which the open-borders policy might wipe out. Time is running out.

Is Europe Trapped in Self-guilt?

SPAIN INVADED CENTRAL America after its native Christopher Columbus discovered the New World, first landing in 1490 in what are now known as the Bahamas Islands. The Spanish conquistadors over the centuries destroyed the Mayan civilization, killing a large proportion of its people, grabbing loads of gold from what is now Peru to ship to Spain. They did the same to two other civilizations, Aztec and Olmec.

During the colonial period (1492-1832), an estimated two million Spaniards settled in America with terrible outcome for the indigenous population. Close to eight million deaths followed the initial conquest.

Use of guns against native civilizations, unaware of firearms, executions after inquisitions and deliberate proliferation of European diseases like plague were the methods employed by the Spaniard conquistadors to carry out this genocide.

Of an original (approximately) 50 million indigenous people in the New World, there were less than two million left a few hundred years later. This is possibly the world's biggest genocide. The provocation for such cruelty is not known, but much of it was sadistic in nature. The angst among present-day Europeans because of this colonial past is, therefore, not difficult to understand.

Portugal followed Spain and conquered the present Brazil, which is the only Latin American nation to speak Portuguese. The rest of South America speaks Spanish. This was Europe's first experiment in enriching itself at the cost of other countries. Further in its history, several European countries went out and captured areas of Africa and Asia and exploited their wealth.

The Netherlands, whose people were natural sailors went mainly to Africa and Asia. Today's South African Afrikaner population has Dutch parentage, and Afrikaans, the language it speaks is similar to Dutch. The Netherlands went further east, held parts of Kerala for several decades, and Sri Lanka too, where their identifiable successors are the Burghers, who are well educated and hold high positions in society.

The richest Dutch prize was today's Indonesia, earlier known as the East Indies. Though not known for extreme cruelty, Dutch colonialism was not devoid of sadism, especially at the lower levels of sailors and soldiers.

France first tried its conquering hand in India, but failed to prevail over British East India Company, though it did meet with success in Vietnam, Cambodia and Laos. In India, the British later left the French alone and allowed them to hold on to Pondicherry, Chandranagar near Calcutta and Mahe on Kerala's western coast. The Portuguese held on to Goa, Daman and Diu, also ruling Angola and Mozambique in Africa. France conquered and retained large territories in northern Africa—notably Senegal and the Arab countries of Morocco, Algeria and Tunisia.

Portuguese cruelty, particularly in converting natives to Roman Catholicism, is well documented. Their mission was mainly religious. The French were more ambitious to spread their proud culture. In Africa, Congo was about the only colony that fell into Belgium's hands. By all accounts, their soldiers were not known to follow a dividing line between cruelty and kindness.

Britain built history's greatest empire, one-fourth of the world's land area upon which the sun never set. While there was no organised violence or cruelty perpetrated on a national scale, sadistic behaviour by British soldiers and young officers was not absent. The Jallianwala Bagh massacre in Amritsar by Brigadier Reginald Dyer is an example. Perhaps one of the most shocking cases was that of a celebrated cavalry regiment, the 9th Lancers, drawn from British aristocracy, and having high and powerful connections. On 9 April 1902, two troopers of the regiment which had arrived in Sialkot from South Africa, asked their native cook Atu to provide them with a woman. His refusal resulted in a savage beatup. The troopers broke two of his ribs, bunged his eyes and rained blows on his head, face, back and chest. Atu was left all night, bleeding and unconscious. He was carried to a hospital only to die nine days later.

An enquiry by the regimental authorities turned out to be a sham, forcing Viceroy Lord Curzon to conclude that it was a crude attempt to hush up the murder. He saw this incident as a travesty of justice, and a crushing blow to British rule.

Such sadism and the colonial experience would have left a scar upon the civilized European conscience. Whether a guilty conscience leaves behind any particular psychological complex or not, one does not know. Nor has any psychologist been known to consider masochism as a reaction to sadism. Sadism is the obtainment of pleasure by imposing agony on others whereas masochism is deriving pleasure through inflicting pain upon oneself. Nevertheless, it is intriguing to see Europe going out of its way to be kind and hospitable to migrants from the old colonies. Latin America is far away and the current migrants have come mainly from the African and Asian colonies. There have been a number of European countries welcoming Islamic immigrants despite the Continent's own experience of Muslim oppression between the year 712 AD and 1681 when the second siege of Vienna ended. Even thereafter, Balkan Europe with its proximity to Turkey has continued experiencing the old Muslim ways.

In the 20th century, Islamists declared a virtual war on Europe at the 1972 Munich Olympic Games, massacring a dozen Israeli athletes. Thereafter, more countries have become victims of terrorism and also incessant Muslim migration. France today has Muslims numbering over ten percent of its population. Germany has a host of Turkish 'guest workers-cum-citizens'. Belgium and Holland are oppressed by migrants from Turkey and Morocco while Spain is a remarkable case. Conquered by the Moors in the eighth century and driving them out only in the fifteenth, it has allowed thousands of Moors back again. Reconquering Christians in Spain had given three choices to the Moors: reconversion, exit or death. How else can one explain this paradoxical conduct than to suspect that the host countries suffer from a psychological complex, whether masochism or any other?

The Muslim encounter with the West dates back to the

beginning of Islam's expansion. The Arab conquest of the Byzantine Empire in Southwest Asia and North Africa led to Eastern Christian churches (Byzantines, Jacobites, Copts, Gregorians, and Nestorians) falling under their control. Reversal of this began with the Crusades and the Reconquista with the fall of Granada in 1492.

According *The Oxford History of Islam*, Europe's current encounter with Islam is a by-product of World War II. A 1986 estimate said about 23 million Muslims were present in Europe. North African and Senegalese mercenaries recruited to fight in French colonial wars were the first to settle in France.

A small number of Muslims have lived in Berlin since 1777. The country is home to temporary 'guest workers' imported to relieve the shortage of manual labour in the post-World War II economic reconstruction. However, the German society's impression that these 'guest workers' would return to their homelands is not materialising. Chancellor Merkel's chant of the 'welkum' mantra notwithstanding, ethnic Germans have become shrill in declaring Muslim presence a threat. It is the same story in other European countries. Hungary, Poland, Austria and now Italy have firmly decided to shut the door on Muslim migration.

Scholar Oswald Spengler's thesis *The Decline of the West* (in 1921) predicted as much. Describing the third phase of a civilizational cycle—growth, flourish and inevitable decline—Egyptian writer Bat Yèor wrote a pamphlet *Eurabia* in 2005 predicting the Arabization of Europe.

The term Eurabia was coined by Bat Yèor in the early 2000s. Her contention is that Europe "has surrendered to Islam and is in a state of submission in which the continent is forced to deny its own culture, stand silently by in the face of

Muslim atrocities, accept Muslim immigration, and pay tribute through various types of economic assistance". According to this theory, the blame rests with a range of groups, including communists, the media, universities and mosques.

Bat Yèor's theory has given rise to anti-Islamic sentiments and movements like "Stop Islamisation of Europe". It gained renewed traction after the 9/11 terror attacks. The prospects of a demographic threat, the fear of an Islamic takeover of Europe sometime in the future, or as the distinguished Islamic scholar Bernard Lewis put it, "Europe will be Islamic by the end of the century", are looming large. Walter Laqueur's *The Last Days of Europe* is quoted often among Eurabia literature.

Why is Europe in Decline?

THE YELLOW VEST agitation continues to bedevil the streets of several French cities. Its major demand is that President Emmanuel Macron must resign. On the one hand, his government is enforcing economies of expenditure by reducing jobs as well as the perks of its many employees. Incidentally, something like 40 percent of the employment in France is, one way or the other, by the State. On the other hand, the Macron government is allowing migrants from West Asia to enter in droves. Inevitably, this has resulted in significant cost. It has meant cuts on the citizens while spending on foreigners who are being welcomed.

A few other countries, such as Germany, have followed this policy of welcome in recent past whereas others like Hungary, Poland, Austria and Italy are openly opposed to West Asian immigrants. There are others which are under financial pressure, like Greece and Portugal, even without immigrants. These are essentially the symptoms of the state of Europe. The disease, if any, is deeper. That Europe could turn into Eurabia within decades has been written about, but evidently no serious notice has been taken by governments. In a number of countries, including in Germany and France, opposition parties are protesting and highlighting their fears of their countries losing their cultures.

What is the disease behind these lackadaisical symptoms? Oswald Spengler, a Munich based scholar, had way back between 1918 and 1922 authored a book called *Der Untergang des Abendlandes* in German, known in English as *Decline of the West.* His contention was that Europe had passed the creative stage of culture and had entered the civilizational phase, in which people are reflective as well as fond of material comfort. The question that arises now is: whether the whole of Europe and all its countries are more in unison when it comes to the progress of history? Are all of them together in the process of decline? How is it that Germany, for example, in the flourish of prosperity which may be giving its government the confidence to take in immigrants, in order to increase hands for manual work, whether unskilled or skilled, behaves the way it currently does?

On the other hand, there are a number of countries fumbling economically that do generally appear in an apparent state of decline. The ethnic white populations across the continent are going down in numbers; hence the readiness to accept immigrants from Asian regions. No study appears to have been made as to who would make congenial settlers and who not. Evidently, those who are conscious of their religious or collective identity would, sooner or later, compete against the 'host countries' specific European culture. Those communities that do not wear their identity on their sleeve, as it were, are culturally safer. Hopefully, they could get absorbed by the local European culture, over say, a generation or two. This also implies that a culture that is conscious of its determination to survive and grow would have to be careful, choosy and possibly assertive at some stage. Whereas the country or culture that is careless or indifferent is either in decline or slated downwards before long. Hungary and Poland for example, have made it clear that they do not want to risk their Christian ethos to be disturbed by an Islamic inflow.

The writer has discussed with a few British citizens as to why their compatriots voted for Brexit when 85 percent of their exports head for the European Union markets. Their unanimous answer was that the motivation of many non-Londoners was the fear of West Asian immigrants. Once a person enters any EU country, he/she is free to travel from Paris to London by train through the undersea Channel, as there is no perceptible barrier at Victoria Station. Britain already has an ample number of Pakistanis; there is no need or space for more of a similar culture. The country has had quite a large number of bomb blasts and other terrorist attacks. The present Mayor of London is a second generation Pakistani, while the East End is full of former Bangladeshis.

At the end of Europe, Moscow has over 25 percent of Muslim population which is strictly speaking not migrants. They settled first in the capital city of the Tsarist empire, which later became the Soviet Union. This is not to indulge in religious prejudice but to be cautious because Islam commands the loyalty of its followers much more staunchly than the devotees of other faiths. They are Muslims first, Muslims second and everything else later. The priority of the country in which they reside is much lower. Nationalism is seldom mentioned in the Muslim's lexicon. Until the end of the 16th century the ideology of the Christian monarchies was also inspired by religion. That ethos began to change with the advent of John Calvin, a Frenchman, and Martin Luther, a Saxon, finding that a great deal of wealth was getting transferred to the Vatican from the outlying areas. The German speaking regions alone sent out about three hundred thousand gold pieces annually.

The reformists pleaded for more emphasis on faith and prayer and less on rituals. Reformation, as the changes were collectively called, spread to other countries like Scotland where the Presbyterian Church came into being. England also ceased to be Roman Catholic and separated to become the Church of England. The exciting cause was that King Henry VIII wanted a divorce from his wife Catherine of Aragon and the Pope expressed his helplessness even to annul the marriage. Since then, the monarch became the head of this Anglican Church. These were not merely religious changes but also reflected the rise of nationalism. Each nation appeared to assert its own identity. They remained the worshippers of Jesus Christ but not all continued to be Roman Catholic. The rise of the Continent and the beginning of European imperialism more or less coincided. Spain and Portugal captured parts of the New World while Holland, France, England and also Portugal went east to establish their colonies in India and also what were broadly called the East Indies.

Soon enough, many a European country was set on the path of exceptional prosperity. By the beginning of 20th century the Continent represented the wealthiest civilization in human history. The secret of its success was nationalism and the resultant competition among the nations as well as among business houses within the countries. The name given to the economic ideology was capitalism whose political consequence, according to Karl Marx, would be war and imperialism. Capitalism was alleged to lead to class exploitation and its reaction was the ideology of communism. The action and the reaction were summed up by Marx as "from each according to his ability to each according to his need". The two big players representing these opposing ideologies were the USA and the Soviet Union. The tussle between the two began after 1917 and ended in 1991 with the collapse of the Soviet Union. Coincidentally, the following year, the European Union was formed as a result of the well known Maastricht Treaty being signed.

Napoleon Bonaparte had dreamt of the United States of Europe before his final defeat at Waterloo in 1815. That was a dream but the reality was a fear of another European war *a la* the two world wars and the human and material exhaustion they caused. These led to a civilizational fatigue. In order to recover, one would have thought the European nations should have returned to their good old tournament of competition which had made them rich and successful. Instead, the Europeans chose to opt out of competition and vote for a cooperative federation of the Continent. Their secret of success, namely competition, was dumped overboard. That was rather like giving up exercise for fitness forever in order to recover from the fatigue of war.

When the writer visited Greece, a taxi driver bitterly criticised his country for joining the European Union. His contention was that even the five fingers of a hand are different and cannot work at the same pace. How does one expect the Mediterranean economies to work at the same pace as the north

European? Greece cannot compete with say, Germany, and is therefore perpetually stretched. All because of the common currency, i.e. the Euro, which yokes together so many varied economies. When Greece's traditional currency the drachma was in operation, it was much easier to function. In the event Greece fell behind, its national bank could devalue the drachma and thus welcome more tourists. Now there is no way except to beg, borrow or go bankrupt.

The choice before all the members of the EU who use the Euro is either to tighten their belts, pull up their socks, catch up with German efficiency and prosper—alternatively huff and puff, hum and haw until the country goes bust.

FROM CRICKET AND SEX TO ASSAM

Parathas and Sex

THIS REPORT FROM Moolchand Metro station (*The Pioneer* 1 September 2018) could do a yeoman's service to our society. Hardly a day passes when the media does not report one rape case or more. Yet few Indians, social scientists included, see a connection between frequent rape crimes and its alleviation, and paid sex, but instead view the latter also as a crime. With continual urbanisation, the number of families living apart has increased. When most people lived in villages or small towns, families lived together. With joint families, the young man's income was not a pressing issue. Hence, early marriages were more a rule and less an exception. The challenge of sex did not normally arise. It led to the crime largely by perverse men.

Even in those easier times, the contempt towards sex outside marriage was largely confined to the middle classes. Amongst the upper rungs of society, whether land based or industry supported, having a mistress was not looked down upon. On the contrary, a wealthy man without a *tawaif* was not usual. In many a society circle in Mumbai before Independence, the measure of a man's status was the quality of his mistress' singing and possibly also dance. A cousin of the writer's grandfather Nathubhai Vora lived most of his life with a lady no other than the famous classical songstress Kesarbai Kelkar, a Padma Vibhushan awardee. An incidental blessing happened to be that he was not married. If any relatives dropped in to call on him, Kesarbai would be around like any other friend.

On the other hand, the working classes did not particularly attach any stigma to extramarital sex. If the farm could not sustain the livehood of a man, he had to go to a city for work. Not everyone could afford housing or even a room for his family. The result was that he lived alone for months on end. He then found release by payment which was altogether preferable to molestation or rape. This crime is only recently being looked upon as dastardly, especially since the tragedy of Nirbhaya. Some have called it beastly but the writer disagrees. Animals or beasts do not rape; the male follows a female when she is on heat and not otherwise. Whether perpetrated in public or in the family, rape is a barbaric act.

On the other hand, the world's oldest profession is not fundamentally very different from a contractual, as distinct from a sacramental marriage. Only the time span varies; some contracts require payment, called *mahr*, at the time of the wedding. An eligible groom is universally an income drawing man. A marriage is sanctified by either a priest or a government official, whereas paid sex is a private mutual arrangement. At the same time, having a *tawaif* was not looked down on, whereas anything confined to a short duration is deemed immoral.

Although one appears not to have questioned the Shia practice of *nikah-e-mut'ah*, which has no minimum time limit. Raja Ghazanfar Ali Khan, who in pre-Independence days was the Dewan of the Kota princely state, was invited with his wife to a special birthday party of the Maharajah. As he did not wish his wife to be seen in public, he contracted a *nikah-e-mut'ah* with a lady apparently for going to the party. The Raja subsequently happened to become an envoy of Pakistan to India. Sir Vidia Naipaul, the Nobel Prize winning famous author, is reported to have been visiting prostitutes in London as reported by his biographer Patrick French, the well known author. This was despite being married to Lady Patricia until her death.

The Vaishali born Amrapali was beautiful and rose to be the *nagarvadhu* or royal courtesan. She was a contemporary of Lord Buddha, who once in response to her invitation, visited her house and dined with her. This incident reflects the social attitude towards courtesans in those times; even the Buddha did not deem it degrading to dine with one. In any case, a number of Hindu temples did have *devadasis* who were sanctified by dancing for the ostensible entertainment of the deities. There are camp followers attached to most militaries, duly approved by the defence authorities.

The contempt perhaps developed after the entry of Christian influence in India. The religion has looked upon sex as a sin to be avoided. Jesus Christ was said to have been born of Immaculate Conception, free from original sin. The Church might be justified in its contention, but if it has moulded our morality, it is unfortunate especially for women in India. This has been unfortunate for both—the girls who are victims of molestation, as well as the poor women who give pleasure for payment. Incidentally, at one time, Europe did recognise prostitute saints. Mary Magdalene was one duly respected by Christianity. Or did the prejudice grow out of dread of contagious diseases?

No doubt, a system of licence should be introduced to give the profession due legitimacy. More importantly, the system would help to protect the health of the women as well as their patrons. And above all, the women would be freed from the frequent harassment they suffer at the hands of the law and order authorities. Strangely enough, it is invariably the women who are arrested and punished. One never hears of any patron being arrested. Why? Because if any law is violated, it must be by both parties. In Kolkata, for long years there is a locality, off the main arterial road Chittaranjan Avenue, called Sonagachi. There are many houses there that are rented by individual women professionals. There is no particular stigma attached to the locality or the practice. One does not hear or read in the papers about raids and arrests made in the area.

The writer grew up in Kolkata and spent 38 years there. He cannot remember any reports during those decades of either rape or molestation. Amongst the middle classes, there was respect for the women. The most affectionate way to address one, even a daughter, is by saying *Maa*. Was it because most Hindus worshipped Durga the most? In all, there are thirteen devi pujas in the year. Was the attitude towards women influenced by this worship of female deities? Some sociologists thought so. There is no doubt that Hinduism is about the only faith which bows to so many female deities. It is eminently shameful, therefore, that there should be so many cases of rape so often.

Paid sex has been widely called the world's oldest profession which means it dates back to many centuries ago when collective human living began—hich means that there has been a universal, permanent need for it. Why then the popular contempt for it? Yet, quite amazingly, there has been no attempt in India to reform or reorganise or in any way to improve its condition. After all, the overwhelming majority of women go into the profession out of sheer poverty. Where is our social conscience? Why not begin by giving the profession legal recognition and then make rules to ensure health, hygiene and fairness? A number of countries in Europe did so years ago.

Gandhi and Currency Notes

RECENTLY A NIECE, her husband and seven-year-old son Soren stayed with us for a few days. They are citizens of Canada and live in Tornoto. In the course of some payments to a home delivery Pizza vendor, Soren happened to see several Indian currency notes. Seeing Gandhiji's portrait on one he wanted to see all the denominations. To his surprise, he found Gandhi's portrait on each note. Who is this person, he asked me. Why is the great man present on every note? I had said that Gandhi was a saintly man. So the youngster asked, was he so very fond of money, that his photograph had to be printed on every bill (as they call notes in America)?

My reply was that he was a saintly man and had little to do with money. He normally lived in an *ashram* or monastery. His great concern was that India should be free from the yoke of the British rule. He wore a simple *dhoti* and in winter a thin woollen shawl. On his feet he wore *chappals* and generally carried a long bamboo stick to balance himself. He ate simple food and drank goat milk in the morning. You mean Soren asked, he did not draw even a salary? Who paid for his food? Wherever he lived, he was fed free, I said. You mean, he had no money in the bank? No, nothing as far I knew was my reply. Oh my God, exclaimed Soren, you think your government imposed all this huge collection of bills on him after he died?

I tried to explain to the child that no one has imposed anything on the great man. It is just that the Indian people adore Gandhi so much that they use his portrait on their currency notes. Soren was not satisfied and he went on. Have you no other great man or woman in your country? Like they have had so many Presidents in the USA. Every sum 5,10,20,50, dollar bills have a different portrait. At this point his father Kevin took over and remarked that our bills did give the impression that Indians were obsessed with Gandhi. Why after so many years, so many billions are focused on the same person? Hardly any one of you has seen him. And India, from what he has read, had a galaxy of freedom fighters—Nehru, Patel, that soldier hero Subhas and so on.

I replied by saying that if you look at our history, you would find a mega-gallery of great men. A professor who happened to come to the house to visit us joined in to insist that we are being extremely unfair to Gandhi. Money was his last concern, nor was he lucky with wealth. In his days, more Indians walked barefoot than with footwear. More young children walked about half naked than fully clothed. We should not involve Gandhi with money, stressed the professor. In fact, he went on, if any of our leaders needs to be remembered for national wealth it was the late Prime Minister Narsimha Rao who released India from the bondage of socialism and made it free to trade and acquire wealth. Finally the professor thumped a table nearby and loudly proclaimed that by printing Gandhi on currency notes we are insulting the great old man. And we appear to be hypocritical to the more perceiving—that we display Gandhi so much and practice nothing of what he stood for. Lately, we have added a reproduction of his round frame spectacles on the same currency notes. What do they symbolise except short-sightedness? What is there to be proud of in that deficiency?

To check on what the young fellow Soren brought up, what I thought and how the professor reacted, I referred the issue to a long retired but a very wise judge. He was quick to opine. For 40 years or so after Independence, we made do with the Ashoka *stambh* or pillar on our notes. There was no human portrait. Then all of a sudden Gandhi's photograph appeared with a vengeance on all denominations. On what provocation, the judge could not guess. His further point was: if the government wanted to spread a noble message or example through the currency, there was a better way.

India has innumerable heroes—ancient, medieval and modern. Why can we not deploy a separate example with each denomination. Say Lord Krishna with his insistence on doing one's duty without looking for its reward. And his insistence on the ruler governing for the country and its people and not for himself; Adi Sankaracharya, the father of a great deal of modern Indian thought and spiritual culture; Ramanuja who propagated *bhakti* through Vedanta; Kabir and his *sahaja-yoga* or simple union, as a secular ideal; Raja Ram Mohan Roy and his anxiety to abolish the evil of *sati*; Swami Vivekananda and his reform like the elimination of child marriage, still quite rampant unfortunately; or his keenness to educate women, his ideals of self perfection and service to society; Sri Aurobindo and his dialectic, cosmic salvation through yoga which transcends reason as well as intuition. Also Netaji Subhas Bose, the hero soldier of Indian freedom whose Azad Hind Fauj convinced the British that more Indians working for their foreign regime might rebel; it was therefore time to leave. Or CV Raman, the nobel Laurate, for his Raman effect—change in the wavelength of light that occurs when a light beam is deflected by molecules. Or Gurudev Rabindranath Tagore.

Or say Kalidas and his legendary play *Meghdoot* and others. Or say Mirza Asadullah Ghalib, the most popular Urdu poet of the 19th century and his famous words: *Ghalib Ka andaz-e-bayan aur* or, *Kaabe per purdah bane rehane do ay Ghalib, kahin wahan bhi kafir sanam na nikale.* Or, Rani Ahilya Bai who ruled Indore with distinction for 30 years and built the road that even now links Jagannathpuri to Kolkata. She was the one ruler who replaced many a monumental temple earlier destroyed by foreign invaders including today's Kashi Vishwanath temple and the mandir at Somnath where the devotees still worship.

Cricket in Need of Revolution

SEVERAL OF US gathered around a TV to see India winning the third Test Match of a series against England. In the second over, A Rashid hit the ball which appeared to be heading to the boundary. Ishant Sharma chased it lazily but saved the four on the edge. My colleagues forgave him; after all they said the match was bound to be won with only the last wicket left. My thoughts flew to 1946 England when India was playing the Surrey county as was customary for a visiting team to do in those days. The match was nearing the end. Chandu Sarwate had come in to bat at number 10 and Shute Banerjee at number 11, both specialist bowlers. To the crowd's astonishment each of them scored a century, a total of 249 between them, before play ended, a record yet unbroken. Never take anything for granted.

A mindset is more comfortable to live with than continual

new thinking. India is an enormous country. All other cricketing nations are comparably smaller. Yet, we have only one competitive international cricket team. The same stars play Test Matches, One-Dayers as well as Twenty-20s. Why? All the three are different formats. In a Test, the bowling is the attack, whether speed or spin. The bowlers' primary function is to take wickets. On his retirement, the judgment on a bowler is based on the total number of Test wickets he took during his career. Seldom is his run average per wicket discussed nor the number of wickets per innings.

When we come to One-Dayers, the bowlers should be looked upon as the defence, not the attack. With the overs limited to 50, the onus of scoring as quickly as possible is on the batsmen. Even all 10 wickets securely saved but with only 150 runs on board is unlikely to win a match. All wickets down but 400 runs on board is far more creditable. In other words, in a 50 overs match, the batsmen have no alternative but to attack sooner or later. Sanath Jayasuriya of Sri Lanka innovated the tactic of hitting out in the first ten overs of power-play when there were field placement restrictions. Moreover, the bowling is fast which makes scoring effortless if the batsman can get his bat to contact the ball. Spinners most often demand greater batting effort.

Most of the time, captains chalk out the batting order as they have done over the decades in Test matches. One-Dayers require much more tactical and flexible batting sequence. Say for example, the first two batsman play well and score 65 runs or more and the going appears good, the captain could gamble on sending in a hard hitting normally number 7 batsman. Without pressure or tension, he might click and score say up to 50 runs. The same player under pressure might not be able to score fluently because he would not have a wide stroke range to safely hit every variety of balls. He is likely to be able to score freely only by hitting out which is not wise when there appears a risk of his team losing. In short, when the traditional good batsmen fail, the burden of recovery falls on the later order players; there are no class batsmen left by then as per the declared order.

The third variety of matches, the Twenty-20 is less cricket and more hit out or get out. Again, bowling would be the defence. The best defensive bowler the writer has seen was Bapu Nadkarni who consistently bowled straight on the stumps, with perfect length but with little guile or spin. It was almost impossible to score runs off his bowling. His record bowling analysis once was 30 overs, 27 maidens, 7 runs and no wickets. That is the ideal bowler for 50 or 20 over matches. For the latter matches, the batsmen selected should be those who can hit the most, no matter the consequences.

Unfortunately, India fields mostly the same so called best players for all three types of games. We overstrain these players and might even be risking the quality of their game. What is worse is that we deny opportunities to many budding cricketers. A large country like ours should have available and ready five top national teams. Say, one team for Tests, two for One-Dayers and two for Tewnty-20. Between them, these teams could tour other countries more frequently as well as host as many visitors as are interested in coming to India. We should no longer treat sports, whether cricket or any other, including athletics, as merely games as in the old days. They should also be looked upon as generators of wealth for the country as well as for the participants and backup services. The more of our youth are enthused to play, the healthier as a nation we would be.

To come back to the technology of cricket, what about the ambidexterity of players? There are quite a few cricketers who bowl with the left arm but bat with the right hand; and vice versa. There are fielders who use one arm while throwing the ball to the wicket-keeper but while batting or bowling they use the other. Herein lies the potential for more versatile players. Wherever a coach sees this phenomenon in a youngster, could he not teach the child, whether a boy or a girl, to bat with both the hands, and similarly bowl or field? A left handed batsman is valuable when it comes to facing an in-swing ball or a googly bowler. Similarly, a left arm bowler is useful against most right handed batsmen. Of course, an ambidextrous player should declare to the umpire which hand or arm he proposes to use in the ensuing over.

Until now, it has been customary for selectors to choose eleven players plus three reserves. But now on they should begin to keep in mind that hypothetically the horizon of their choice is 52 and not 11 players, plus a captain. They could begin gradually avoiding those players who are not all-rounders. Just as for some years now, poor fielders are not chosen. The author remembers overhearing a conversation, in the corridor of Elphinstone College, Mumbai in 1954, among Subhash Gupte, the outstanding googly bowler, and his cronies. One of them had asked Gupte as to why he never chased a ball and allowed it to travel to the boundary. His answer in simple Marathi was, "If I chase balls to save boundaries, who do you think would do the googly bowling? I would get too tired." In those days out-fielding was considered the function of the non-bowlers only. Nor was a catch a catch unless it came spontaneously into a fielder's hand.

The writer happened to be present when once Syed Mushtaq Ali, the charismatic opening batsman of the 1940s and early

50s, spoke to people present in a sports club tent on the Kolkata Maidan. One of his remarks was that we Indians are satisfied if we can gather six good batsmen, four steady bowlers and a wicket-keeper. If there happened to be two or three all-rounders among them, they were a bonus. But that was not so in England and Australia, he said. The selectors in these countries deliberately looked out for all-rounders and insisted on reliable fielders. Every player had to have at least two merits—either bowler batsman or if only one, then a good fielder.

Happily, we Indians have a come a long way since then. Now let us try to have five merits in a player—both arm bowling and both hand batting plus the present standard of fielding. If we can produce one or two such versatile players, many others would follow the example. And we would witness yet another revolution.

Homeopathic Reservations

THE INCORPORATION OF the demand of the Maratha community for 16 percent reservation will take Maharashtra's percentage of reservations to 68, well in excess of the 50 percent ceiling laid down by the Supreme Court. Tamil Nadu already has 69 percent of its government jobs under the reserved category. Both the states have exceeded the Supreme Court stipulation that 50 percent should be the ceiling for reservations. The balance 50 at least should be left free for open competition. The apex court had ruled in 1969 that reservations cannot exceed 50%. However, there are state laws that exceed this limit and these are under litigation in the Supreme Court. For example, the caste based reservation stands at 69% and is applicable to about 87% of the population in the state of Tamil Nadu.

Reservation has been an enticing political fruit which is

not as sweet as it was believed to be. And it has been becoming blander by the years. With the liberalisation of the economy in 1991, government jobs have been reducing and new public sector corporations are not being set up. Yet, politically, the colour of the fruit has grown more and more attractive. Years ago, the Gujjars agitated for getting a percentage, much later the Jats, then came the Patel demands in Gujarat, and thereafter was the intense follow up by the Marathas. All these are forward castes and have a substantial say in the governments of their respective states. Marathas hold an electoral de facto veto in Maharashtra, like the Jats in Haryana, the Gujjars in Rajasthan and the Patels in Gujarat. Moreover, the distinguished sociologist MN Srinivas and his theory of caste sanskritisation among the Hindus would not accept anyone demoting his community's status. Every Hindu ideally desires to go up the ladder. No caste or a section of it wishes to go down the ladder. What then is the secret motivation behind these four upper castes demanding to be OBC's or other backward castes?

Uncannily, reservations were first introduced neither by politicians nor by the Constitution but, in his state, by the Maharaja of Kolhapur as early as in 1902. Reportedly, the princely states of Baroda and Mysore were already practising reservations although Kolhapur was the first to issue a written government order. A British seal was first put on the concept of reservation when, as part of the Morley-Minto Reforms, the Government of India Act 1909 was passed by the Westminster Parliament. Dr BR Ambedkar, who headed the drafting committee for the Constitution favoured a ten year reservation for the depressed castes as well as the tribals. This proposal found support from generally everyone. As far as the other castes are concerned, it all began with the appointment of the

Mandal Commission in 1979 for finding out which were the Other Backward Castes (OBC). This term OBC was first used in the census of 1931 which recorded a total of 1,257 such castes across India.

Is it a possibility that these non-OBC sons and daughters do not always get a job on merit? On the other hand, OBC youngsters walk away with the same jobs because of their caste. The latest attempt to join the OBC club may be their response to the challenge. Could the third possibility be a homeopathic treatment to remove or render redundant something they have grown up to disapprove of? Homeopathic means sympathetic treatment or aggravating the symptoms until they get ejected from the body. The normal approach is antagonistic treatment or to attack the symptoms of the disease which is the allopathic, the ayurvedic or the Unani method.

The homeopathic strategy, if at all, could be to provoke yet other castes to also demand reservation until the percentage becomes so large as to become farcical. That would leave very little or no scope for the general or non-reserved category that the system of reservation could expire. It is widely recognised that no government is likely to have the courage to abolish reservation. This is illustrated by the scheduled caste and tribe categories which were to enjoy reservation for ten years only till say, 1960. And yet, they are still carrying on. A Jat and a Patel leader each has mentioned in the writer's presence that he and his colleagues are embarrassed to ask for reservation. But what else to do, was their question.

Several other questions can arise as one thinks further. Nehruvian socialism was the picnic period or the halcyon era of reservations. The bureaucracy was expanding at both the Centre and the State levels. At the same time, one PSU after another was being established. In other words, jobs where reservation was available were virtually an expanding torrent. In the same decades, banks were nationalised, as were the general insurance companies and the entire coal industry. Liberalisation-cum-globalisation introduced in 1991 overturned this apple cart. Parallel to this was the realisation by the State governments that most of their public sector corporations were also losing money by the day. Since then, reserved seats or vacancies have been shrinking. Until now the official spokesmen have used the Indian saying, 'whichever country's government is a trader its people are going to be beggars". Or there is the other slogan: "maximum governance with minimal government". On top of all this is the fact that not only is the computer reducing routine jobs in industry but also the Sword of Damocles of the robot is hanging over everyone's head.

Yet another question would be an upper caste backlash. How that may shape up, if at all, needs to be seen. But a political example was the fall of the Madhavsinh Solanki ministry in 1986. He had gone flat out on backing the OBC's in his choice of candidates for the Assembly elections of 1985. He won hands down and secured 146 MLAs out of the total of 182. The upper caste reaction was so severe that by 1986, he was thrown out of power and replaced by an Adivasi Amarsinh Chaudhry as the head of Gujarat government. Finally, in the long run, excessive reservations could lead to a brain drain of the country, as has happened in Tamil Nadu. Many a Brahmin has migrated either overseas or to other parts of India.

All the disadvantages apart, the question arises: what are the benefits of reservations? True, they are excellent for political promising. But the actual boons of the scheme need to be surveyed. Do the beneficiaries pass around the gains to their communities? Or do they merely look after their families only? If that be so, is this advantage sufficient to offset the demoralisation they cause amongst the castes who are left out? And often there is a decline in the quality of the service the several candidates give to the society generally or to the concerned individuals particularly. In the bargain, society does not make the progress at the speed it is capable of. A nationwide debate on the pros and cons of reservation is called for. This discussion should not exclude the Muslims and Christians, on behalf of whom reservations have been asked for by some political parties. These religions have foreign origins and they never had any system of caste. Most of the Hindus who converted to these religions did so to escape the oppression of casteism. The question of their sharing the reservations does not, therefore, arise.

Happiness to Assam

FOR A GOOD century and a quarter, Assam has lived under a dual threat of its culture and ethos being marginalised. On occasions, the threat came from immigrants whose language would overshadow the indigenous tongue. And there were times when there were deliberate designs to reduce the sons of the soil to a religious minority. It has been a tale of continual tension caused by neighbours to the south and frequent anxiety emanating from friends in the west. The Assamese could not always be sanguine that its own sons were not playing the sly role enabling the neighbours who were short of fertile land to till and live off their land. A threat engineered and egged on by persons within is worse than a danger posed by antagonists without.

The anxiety among the Assamese people at the passing of the Citizenship (Amendment) Act, is wholly understandable.

Merely assuring the people that protecting their culture is as much the Centre's concern as securing the culture of the entire country does not satisfy. For several good reasons, Assam is a very special and distinct case. For one, Assam and Bangladesh share a border. It is, therefore, most convenient for immigrants to cross over. Since the turn of the 19th into the 20th century, there was infiltration especially from Mymensingh district into the Brahmaputra Valley. From Sylhet into Cachar district a crossover is even easier as they were twin districts pre-partition. The two formed the legendary Surmah Valley.

Unless one has lived or frequently travelled in Assam, it is difficult to appreciate what nightmares the Assamese see when they think of infiltration. They are a gentle people with a soft peace-loving nature. They have their own festivals.

They were gifted by nature with plenty of land and even more rivers and water. They do not have to work too hard for survival. The climate is mostly warm and humid and not congenial for hard work. They are not competitive by nature and understandably shudder at the fear of this ethos being disturbed by outsiders.

Believe it or not, until two decades ago, it was a popular impression that the Congress strategy for winning elections in Assam was "Ali, Coolie and Bengali". Coolie implied the tea garden workers and their families. Ali and Bengali are self explanatory; they are mostly people who had over the years immigrated into Assam. Even the tea garden workers were Adivasis brought from Jharkhand and neighbouring areas to plant and pluck the bushes. To this day, it is difficult to find an original Assamese who is a plucker in a tea garden. In sum and substance, the Congress depended on settlers from outside to win it a majority vote.

Earlier a near fatal game was played with Assam. As mentioned, they are a gentle people. When World War II broke out in Europe, the British also declared that India was a participant. The Congress leaders expressed their grave disapproval for the government doing so without consulting the Indian leaders. In a loud protest, all Congress provincial ministries resigned forthwith, as did the one in Assam. It was replaced by a Muslim League ministry led by Muhammed Saddullah. The idea of Pakistan was already floating in the political air by then. Saddullah concocted a new theory that the Adivasis in Assam were animists and not Hindus. The resulting arithmetic made the Muslims within striking distance of a majority.

In 1947, MA Jinnah nearly convinced the British rulers in New Delhi that Assam was a Muslim majority province and should therefore go to Pakistan. Sheikh Mujibur Rahman, in his book *Eastern Pakistan*, stated that the tribals were not only not Hindus but also unfit for civilised life. The generally vague conclusion of the sympathisers for Pakistan was that Eastern Bengal and Assam should be combined into one province as was the case under the first partition of Bengal by Viceroy Lord Curzon in 1905. Fortunately, it was undone by 1911. Lord Pethic Lawrence, Secretary of State for India, and also one of the three members of the Cabinet Mission 1946, sent by the British government to find out what structure would be accepted to Indian leaders, also swallowed this theory about an amalgamation of the two.

It was touch and go when Gopinath Bordolai, the Assam Congress leader rushed to New Delhi and persuaded those in power and influence that the Jinnah contention was untrue. As a result, Assam was saved for India except for Sylhet district, which is now in Bangladesh. That is the kind of price Assam nearly paid for allowing illegal migrants to settle. Incidentally, until 1874, Assam was a part of the Bengal Presidency. It was then separated and placed under the rule of a Chief Commissioner. To make Assam a viable separate province, three Bengali speaking districts of the Presidency, namely, Goalpara, Sylhet and Cachar were merged into the new province. That is how Assam became not only separate but also began its joint walk in company with Bengalis as well as Muslims. The going of Sylhet to East Pakistan in 1947 relieved this pressure to an extent.

Nevertheless, the partition added Bengalis to the population as Sylhet had been a sister district of Cachar and its people were at least 46 percent Hindu. Moreover, Mymensingh district was also nearby to enable refugees to cross over. Due to the poverty of the landless peasants, Muslim infiltration also continued. West Pakistan monopolised the country's power and the eastern wing was treated as a colony. Emigration was perhaps the only way many an easterner could survive. The poorest came to Assam as well as West Bengal. The more resourceful went to England and other richer countries. Called Bangladeshis since 1971, they have the reputation of being the world's number one migrants in recent decades. No state in India has been spared by their visitation. The writer's temporary gardener at Cochin (now Kochi) turned out to be from Bangladesh. Delhi has any number of domestic servants, many albeit with Hindu pen-names.

Assam, however, can ill afford to host these infiltrators; the Assamese population is so small. The recent Citizenship (Amendment) Bill is a major irritant for them especially since what was discovered in 1979. Some young men discovered in the electoral rolls of the Mangaldai assembly constituency that many a voter was an obvious infiltrator. In order to spread the protest and try and stop such distortion of the electoral rolls of the State, the All Assam Students Union (AASU) was formed. Some members also went on to establish the Assam Ganatantra Parishad (AGP), a major political party. A few members took to terrorism under the name of the United Liberation Front of Assam (ULFA).

The Citizenship (Amendment) Bill has understandably upset the people of Assam in the light of the events just narrated. The fear is that many a Hindu from Bangladesh may take advantage of this legislation and come over to Assam. Such a legal migration would reduce the percentage of the ethnic Assamese and dilute their indigenous culture. On one hand the Bill is welcome because many of the illegal infiltrators who came 1971 onwards can be sent away. But in their place many a legal migrant may come. The dilution of the local culture and the threat to the political voice of the Assamese would be about the same. Hence the disturbed mood not only in Assam but also in the other northeastern states.

The solution to this potentially very serious national problem would lie in making the Cachar district a separate Union Territory having no special political connection with Assam. Cachar has a population of some 40 lakh of whom a little over half are Hindu, under two percent are Christian and the rest Muslim. More or less, all speak and write Bengali. Its economy is viable especially with the help of over a hundred tea gardens which produce five crore kilograms of tea worth some 800 crore rupees annually. That would separate some 16 percent of the total Assam population, virtually all of them Bengali or Muslim; a great relief to the Assamese. Remotely perhaps, the Bodos also may use the chance as an example and also demand a Union Territory of much less than two million people living between Kokrajhar town and Sankosh